★ INSIGHT GUIDES

BARCELONA
Step by Step

APA PUBLICATIONS L

Part of the Langenscheidt Publishing Group

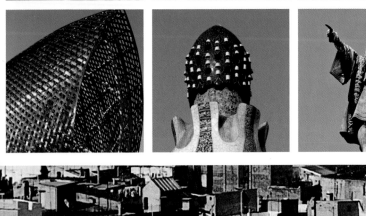

CONTENTS

ABOUT THIS BOOK

This *Step by Step Guide* has been produced by the editors of Insight Guides, whose books have set the standard for visual travel guides since 1970. With top-quality photography and authoritative recommendations, this guidebook brings you the very best of Barcelona in a series of 20 tailor-made tours.

WALKS AND TOURS

The tours in the book provide something to suit all budgets, tastes and trip lengths. As well as covering Barcelona's many classic attractions, the routes track lesser-known sights and up-and-coming areas; there are also excursions for those who want to extend their visit outside the city.

The tours embrace a range of interests, so whether you are an art fan, an architecture buff, a gourmet, a lover of flora and fauna or have kids to entertain, you will find an option to suit.

We recommend that you read the whole of a tour before setting out. This should help you to familiarise yourself with the route and enable you to plan where to stop for refreshments –

Above from top: museum signs, advertising the Museu Marítim; sunbathing on the waterfront boardwalk; the elegant Catalan Renaissance-style arches of the Plaça del Rei; stylish light in Antoni Gaudí's La Pedrera.

options for this are shown in the 'Food and Drink' boxes, recognisable by the knife and fork sign, on most pages.

For our pick of the walks by theme, consult Recommended Tours For… *(see pp.6–7).*

ORIENTATION

The tours are set in context by this introductory section, giving an overview of the city to set the scene, plus background information on food and drink and shopping. A succinct history timeline in this chapter highlights the key events that have shaped Barcelona over the centuries.

DIRECTORY

Also supporting the tours is the Directory chapter, comprising a user-friendly, clearly organised A-Z of practical information, our pick of where to stay while you are in the city and select restaurant listings; these eateries complement the more low-key cafés and restaurants that feature within the tours themselves and are intended to offer a wider choice for evening dining.

The Author

Roger Williams came to know and love Barcelona during frequent visits to the city from his home on the Costa Brava. He is continually delighted by its contradictions and describes it as a city that is at once one of the most bourgeois in the world and also one of the most avant-garde. He illustrates this by describing a scene he witnessed during the rush-hour one morning on La Rambla: 'Walking towards me was a man in a grey jacket, shirt and tie with a briefcase under his arm. His haircut was trim, a little grey at the temples. He was as middle-aged and middle-class as me, but as he passed I looked down and noticed his short tight blue skirt. Only in Barcelona, I thought.'

Feature Boxes
Notable topics are highlighted in these special boxes.

Margin Tips
Shopping tips, quirky anecdotes, historical facts and interesting snippets help visitors to make the most of their time in the city.

Key Facts Box
This box gives details of the distance covered on the tour, plus an estimate of how long it should take. It also states where the route starts and finishes, and gives key travel information such as which days are best to do the route or handy transport tips.

Route Map
Detailed cartography shows the itinerary clearly plotted with numbered dots. For more detailed mapping, see the pull-out map slotted inside the back cover.

Food and Drink
Recommendations of where to stop for refreshment are given in these boxes. The numbers prior to each café/restaurant name link to references in the main text. Places recommended en route are also plotted on the maps. Note that in Spain, addresses marked 's/n' have no house number.

The € signs given in each entry reflect the approximate cost of a two-course meal for one, with half a bottle of house wine. These should be seen as a guide only. Price ranges, which are also quoted on the inside back flap for easy reference, are as follows:

€€€€ €60 and above
€€€ €30–60
€€ €20–30
€ €20 and below

Footers
The footers on left-hand pages give the itinerary name, plus, where relevant, a map reference; those on the right-hand pages cite the main attraction on the double page.

ARCHITECTURE

From pure Catalan Gothic around the Royal Palace (walk 2) to the Modernista showcases of the Eixample (walk 10), including Barcelona's greatest work-in-progress, the Sagrada Família (walk 11).

RECOMMENDED TOURS FOR...

ART BUFFS

Artistic highlights include the Museu Picasso (walk 5) and Monjuïc's Fondacío Miró (walk 12); the latter tour also visits the Palau Nacional, home to the best collection of Romanesque art in the world. For the lowdown on Salvador Dalí, there is a trip to Figueras (tour 19).

FAMILIES WITH KIDS

There is lots to appeal, including the wax museum (walk 1), the boating lake in Parc de la Ciutadella (walk 8), the beach (walk 9), Barça football club (tour 13) and CosmoCaixa science museum and Tibidabo funfair (walk 16).

FLORA AND FAUNA

For a spot of greenery, visit the Parc de la Ciutadella (walk 8), the various gardens on hilly Montjuïc (walk 12) or, for a wilder outdoor experience, go hiking in the mountains around Montserrat (tour 20).

FOOD AND DRINK

Sample the excellent tapas on and around the Passeig de Gràcia (walk 10) or slip up to Gràcia (walk 15) for a drink in one of the area's many authentic local bars. Trips further afield include a tour of the wine region (tour 18).

MUSIC LOVERS

El Liceu opera house (walk 1) and the gorgeous Modernista Palau de la Música Catalana (walk 4) should be top of your list. Also recommended is the wonderful new music museum, the Museu de la Música (walk 8), north of Parc de la Ciutadella.

NIGHT OWLS

You will find places that open late across the city, but good starting points for night-time action include El Born (walk 5) and La Rambla (walk 1), which is busy day and night.

RAINY DAYS

Sit it out in the larger institutions such as the Museu d'Art Contemporani de Barcelona and the Centre de Cultura Contemporània de Barcelona (walk 6) or the Museu Nacional d'Art de Catalunya, in the Palau Nacional (walk 12), or combine shopping at the waterfront Maremàgnum mall with a visit to the aquarium (walk 7).

ROMANCE

Buy flowers on La Rambla (walk 1), take a boat trip on a Golondrina (walk 7) or watch the pretty, illuminated waters of the Font Màgica de Montjuïc (walk 12).

SPORTY TYPES

Visit the buildings erected for the 1992 Olympics (walk 12) or pay homage to Barça football club at Camp Nou (walk 13).

ORIENTATION

An overview of Barcelona's geography, customs and culture, plus illuminating background information on food and drink, shopping, architecture and history.

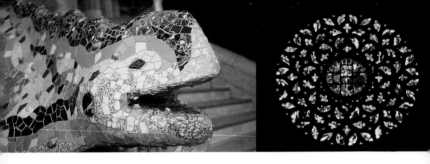

CITY OVERVIEW

A vibrant, dynamic city, always on the move but passionately guarding its heritage, Barcelona offers everything from Gothic treasures and traditional dances to trendy bars, innovative architecture and gorgeous food.

Above: port cable car; Modernista sign; Tibidabo funfair.

Late Habits
Everything starts late in Barcelona: lunch is not usually until 2pm and dinner not until at least 9pm or 10pm, which is when most concerts start. Live-music venues and clubs do not get going until 2am. Pace yourself with a few tapas.

Right: Mercat de Santa Caterina.

When anyone asks what are the best things to see in Barcelona, the answer should always be: just walk the streets. Few cities in the world are so agreeable for simply wandering, thanks to Barcelona's rich architectural heritage, from giant Roman stones and sunless medieval lanes to the brilliant architecture of Gaudí and the Modernistas, and the shimmering, sharp-edged 21st-century blocks that are placed with such panache alongside the historical gems.

DEVELOPMENT

Lying on the Mediterranean coast in north-east Spain, some 260km (160 miles) from France and a distance of 625km (390 miles) from Madrid, Spain's second-largest city was founded by the Romans. The *oppidum* of Barcino was entrenched behind walls encircling the area around what is now the cathedral and the government buildings of Plaça de Sant Jaume. During medieval times – Catalonia's Golden Age – the Counts of Barcelona pushed the walls south beyond the famous La Rambla avenue, to encompass El Raval and create what is now the whole of the old town, or Ciutat Vella. Beyond this lay the hillside Jewish burial grounds of Montjuïc.

The 19th Century

Towards the end of the 19th century a vast new extension (Eixample) was laid out in an impeccable grid system inland, while an industrial area spread north alongside the shore. The Ciutat Vella, the Eixample (where Antoni Gaudí's Sagrada Família and many of the Modernista showcase buildings are located) and the former industrial area

that has been transformed into a beachfront (Barceloneta and the port) are the three key areas that most visitors come to explore.

NAVIGATING THE CITY

Centred on the Plaça de Catalunya that separates the old part of town from the new, Barcelona is an easy city to navigate. The grid system of the Eixample is simple to follow, and though the lanes of the Ciutat Vella are more mazelike, that is half the fun. A good way to get to know your way around is to take a ride on the tourist bus, which passes all the main sights, where you can hop on and off. Taking a trip around the port in a Golondrina pleasure boat is another way to get a sense of the city, while cable cars and funiculars whisk you up to its high spots for bird's-eye views.

If you head up to the castle at the top of Montjuïc, you can see the city stretching far to the south, beyond the commercial port, down to the Llobregat river. In the other direction, heading north, if you walk the whole length of the beach you will eventually arrive at the new Forum and the river Bésos, marking the city's northern edge. The Serra Collserola, with Tibidabo's Sagrat Cor church pricking the skyline, stops the city from expanding far inland.

Public Transport

The transport system, including a highly efficient metro network, is straightforward to navigate. Metro, rail and bus services are all paid for using the same tickets, which are compara-

tively inexpensive, especially if you buy them in blocks of 10. For more information on this, consult the Directory chapter *(see p.111).*

THE BARRIOS

In spite of the city's size, the communities and villages that make up Barcelona give it an intimate feel. These *barrios* (districts) have strong identities and flavours, celebrating their own festivals and making their own entertainment, for example. Usually

Above from far left: salamander in Park Güell; window of Santa Maria del Pi; boarders at the Museu de Art Contemporani de Barcelona; cosy neighbourhood bar.

Population
The population of metropolitan Barcelona is about 3 million.

Below: bird's-eye view from the Sagrada Família.

Busy Barcelonans

The phrase Vaig de bòlit, meaning 'I'm speeding', is used by busy Barcelonans, who live with what George Orwell called 'a passionate energy'. They like to be viewed as *espavilat*: dynamic, assertive and productive.

Below: stylish local walking her dog.

centred on a square or two, where the outdoor seating that is common in Barcelona – with a mild climate and temperatures rarely falling below 10°C (50°F) in winter, and rising to 25°C (77°F) in summer, it is not surprising that people spend much of their time outdoors – allows people to stop for a chat, these *barrios* maintain their individuality. Wherever you stay in the city, you are likely to quickly find a favourite street or square with a bar or café where regulars gather for a morning *cortado* (coffee) or lunchtime *copa* (ice cream) And you will soon find yourself slipping into the rhythm of late starts

(shops open around 10am), quiet afternoons and buzzing early evening, when everyone seems to be out and about for a stroll in the city's streets.

STRONG HERITAGE

Like the city's numerous long-established cafés and bars, many shops seem rooted to the past. It is hard to think of a major city that maintains so many specialist shops: a *polleria* selling nothing but chicken; a *cuchillería* selling knives, a *colmado* that stocks only dried goods. The influx of immigrants has only added to this mix. The city's commercial individuality is borne out, too, with the modern boutiques and one-off designer outlets of El Raval and El Born, where small premises are often just a workshop with a window.

CREATIVE SPIRIT

Diseny (design) is the most pervasive talent in a city that has produced some explosive creativity, in both the plastic and performing arts. The national characteristic is said to be a mix of *seny* (wisdom) and *rauxa* – a kind of wildness that produces creativity. It results in a mix of deep conservatism and mercurial flair, which might explain the Sagrada Família, an extraordinary avant-garde work by a deeply religious traditionalist. It perhaps also explains the city's history, a mix of highs and lows, of times of great prosperity and times of gruelling hardship, times of enlightened thinking and times of incendiary passion.

URBAN PLANNING

The city's urban planning is a match for its architectural bravura. Barcelona is a city whose planners take bold steps, in spite of frequent opposition. They are unafraid to pull down great chunks of old properties and replace them with cutting-edge modern buildings, or simply leave breathing spaces.

Growth Spurts

The city has grown in bursts: the Golden Age of the 13th and 14th centuries produced the Gothic mansions of the Old Town (Ciutat Vella). The architectural development was low-key until the 19th-century industrial boom funded the Modernista extravaganza of the Eixample quarter.

In the mid-20th century, however, the fascist dictator General Franco came along and put a stop to just about everything. In the second half of the 20th century, while other European cities were ripping out their architectural heritage and throwing up skyscrapers, Barcelona languished, unloved by the holders of the national purse strings.

Perversely, this played a major role in saving much of its heritage. But the city's ability to knuckle down and work made its industries hum, and people flocked here from far poorer parts of Spain. When the tourist boom arrived in the 1960s, it was the coast, notably stretches of the Costa Brava to the north, that had to meet the holiday-makers' demands for quickly erected concrete blocks, while Barcelona retained its architectural integrity.

Olympic Renaissance

In fact it was not until 1986 and the prospect of the Olympic Games that the city reawakened, attracting architects of the highest calibre, including its own home-grown practitioners and planners, in a second *reaixença* (renaissance). The confidence and verve with which they attacked Barcelona was breathtaking, and its legacy is a city that is exciting to be in, easy to move around and a pleasure to experience.

Above from far left: waterside restaurants and boats in the port; architect Antoni Gaudí; sculpture by Joan Miró, at the Fundació of the same name; the busy Passeig de Gràcia in the Eixample quarter.

Festivals and Partying

The Barcelonans like to party, and barely a month goes by without some excuse for a party. Each district's *festa major* (main festival) involves large family meals, dishes and pastries created specially for the occasion, plus crates of cava and music. The city's principal festival is the week-long La Mercè in September, with spectacular parades of 'giants', 'dragons' and 'devils' with music and dance and fireworks. In addition to this the festive calendar is marked with celebrations at Carnival, just before Lent, and the eve of the Feast of St John, on 23 June. Two peculiarly Catalan contributions to the party scene are the traditional *sardana* dance (see p.36) and *castells*, human 'towers' that reach five people high. More tranquil is the celebration of St George, patron of Catalonia, when red roses and books are given as gifts (see p.43).

FOOD AND DRINK

Barcelonans are serious about their food. 'Where did you eat?' they will ask with uncharacteristic interest, and your reply will mark you out either as a person of taste and distinction or as someone who needs taking in hand.

Market Meals
The Mercat de la Concepció *(see p.69)* offers daily recipes on its internet site, enabling you to recall the flavours of Barcelona long after your visit. See www. laconcepcio.com for details.

Catalan cuisine is an ancient Mediterranean style of cooking, characterised by the aromas of mountain herbs, the oils and the juices of the plains, the wild meat of the woods and skies, and the flesh of the fish and crustaceans of the sea. *Mar i muntanya* (sea and mountain) is how it is described, a special mixture of seafood and meat.

Many other cuisines can be tried in Barcelona, and there is certainly no shortage of places to eat. The smarter restaurants in the Eixample may have some of the best food, but they tend to lack the personality of restaurants in the Old Town, where classic establishments such as Agut, Caracoles and Set Portes increasingly rub shoulders with newer, trendier places.

Most bars (or *tabernas*, *bodegas* and *cervecerías*, the last meaning 'beer hall') also serve food, often of a surprisingly high standard. Here you can sample tapas, sandwiches (*bocadillos* in Castilian, *bocats* or *entrepans* in Catalan) or *plats combinats* (single-course meals) at almost any time of the day.

MAIN MEALS

Local people usually have an early breakfast of *café con leche* (milky coffee, *cafè amb llet* in Catalan) accompanied by toast or biscuits. Around 11am it is time for a second breakfast, which tends to be a more substantial sandwich or chunky wedge of potato omelette, and pastries.

Late Lunch, Late Dinner
At other meal times, Barcelonans, like all Spaniards, eat late. Lunch usually is not eaten until 2 or 3pm. Dinner is served from about 9pm until 11.30pm, although at weekends people sometimes do not sit down to dinner until midnight. You can usually get a meal at almost any time of the day, but if you enter a restaurant soon after the doors have swung open, you are likely to find yourself dining alone, or with other foreign visitors. To last between lunch and dinner, do as the locals do and fill up on sandwiches and cakes in the patisseries around 5.30pm, or tapas in the bars from 7pm.

COURSES AND FIXED-PRICE MENUS

Barcelonans often eat a three-course meal at both lunch and dinner, including dessert and coffee. However, it is not uncommon to share a first course, or to order *un sólo plato* – just a main course. Many restaurants offer a lunchtime *menú del día* or *menú de la casa*, a daily set menu that gen-

erally offers excellent value for money. For a fixed price you will get three courses: a starter, often soup or salad, a main dish, and dessert (ice cream, a piece of fruit or the ubiquitous *flan* (*flam* in Catalan, a kind of caramel custard), plus wine, beer or bottled water, and bread. Typically, the cost is about half of what you would expect to pay if you ordered the same dishes *à la carte*. Many Spaniards order the *menú*, so there is no need to think you are getting the 'tourist special'.

What to Eat

A typical dinner might begin with *amanida catalana*, a salad with cold meats; or *escalivada*, baked peppers and aubergines, skinned, covered in oil and eaten cold; or *esqueixada*, a salad with shredded cod. A main course could be *suquet* (fish stew) or *estofat* (meat stew), or *botifarra amb mongetes* (sausage and beans), or rabbit *(conill)*, served with snails *(cargols)* or a garlicky alioli sauce.

When it comes to dessert, *crema catalana* (egg custard with caramelised sugar on top) is a highlight. *Mel i mato* is another treat, made with honey and creamy cheese. The best sweets are generally the delicacies sold in pastry shops.

TAPAS AND RACIONS

Tapas (*tapes* in Catalan) – the snacks for which Spanish bars and cafés are

Above from far left: beer and *jamón*; *xurros*; fish restaurant in the port; enticing fresh produce.

Chocolate

If you like chocolate, you are in the right place. You can drink *xocolata desfeta,* chocolate thick enough to stand a spoon up in (great for dipping *xurros* pastries into), see fantastic festive creations and eat main dishes of such unusual combinations as chocolate with rabbit or squid – apparently a traditional combination. Well-established chocolate makers include the Escribà family, with a shop on La Rambla (no. 83), and elsewhere you can find it in raw, brick-sized lumps. New and inventive chocolate makers are increasingly moving in. Visit Cacao Sampaka (Carrer Ferran 43–5 or Carrer Consell de Cent 292) to try their handmade bars, sauces and creams. Or taste chocolate beer and buy chocolate candles at Xocoa (Carrer Petrixol 11; www.xocoa-bcn.com). At Plaça Sant Gregori Taumaturg in the Eixample the award-winning Oriol Balaguer has further delights (www.oriolbalaguer.com). And to find out how it all started, stroll down to the Museu de la Xocolata (Chocolate Museum, see p.45).

Paella and Fideuá

Although it originates in rice-growing Valencia, the classic seafood dish of paella is high on many visitors' lists of dishes to sample in Barcelona. Try the restaurants in Barceloneta for a paella of fresh mussels, clams, shrimp and several kinds of fish. It will take about 20 minutes to prepare. Another delicacy is *fideuá*, which is similar to paella but made with noodles instead of rice.

El Bulli

Voted the world's top restaurant, El Bulli (www.elbulli.com), two hours north of Barcelona at Roses on the Costa Brava, is open only from April to October and has to be booked around 12 months in advance. For the rest of the year owner-chef Ferran Adrià, called 'the Salvador Dalí of the kitchen' by *Gourmet* magazine, works with his chefs in their Barcelona workshop, El Taller, in Carrer de la Portaferrissa just off La Rambla, concocting dishes for a 30-course tasting menu for the following season.

world-famous – come in dozens of delicious varieties, from appetisers such as olives and salted almonds, to vegetable salads, fried squid, garlicky shrimps, lobster mayonnaise, meatballs, spiced potatoes, wedges of omelette, sliced sausage and cheese. The list is endless, and can be surprisingly creative, especially at the now extremely popular Basque tapas joints, where they are called *pintxos*.

A dish larger than a *tapa* is called a *porcion*. A complete serving, meant to be shared, is a *racion*, and half of this, a *media racion*. Tapas are usually available throughout the day, and provide a great way to sample new dishes.

They can also be filling, especially when eaten with a chunk of Catalonia's best invention, *pa amb tomàquet*, bread rubbed with garlic, olive oil and tomato. This bread is particularly good, too, with ham *(pernil)*, spicy sausage *(xoriço)*, cheese *(formatge)* or anchovies *(anxoves)*.

Other dishes to point to on the bar might be *truites*, *tortilla* (Spanish omelette, made with potato and onion, and sometimes also with spinach); small fried fish; octopus; snails; or *patates braves*, potatoes in a hot tomato sauce.

DRINKS

Wine, Cava and Beers

Wine is a constant at the Catalan table. In addition to a wide assortment of fine wines from across Spain, including Rioja, Navarra and Ribera del Duero, Barcelona has some extremely good regional wines. Those from Penedès, the grape-growing region just outside Barcelona where cava, Spain's sparkling wine, is produced, are excellent *(see pp.92–3)*. Cava itself goes wonderfully with seafood and most tapas. Among Penedès reds, try Torres Gran Coronas, Raimat and Jean León.

Wines from the Priorat area, around an hour to the south of Barcelona (near Tarragona), are superb, robust, expensive reds that rival the best in Spain. Do not be surprised to be offered red wine *(vi negre)* chilled in hot weather. There are also several delicious, dry rosés *(vi rosat)* from the region.

Spanish beers, which are available in bottles and on draft, are generally light and refreshing.

Other Alcoholic Drinks

Sangría, made of wine and fruit fortified with brandy, is drunk more by visitors than local people. More popular among the locals is sherry *(jerez)*, of which you will find every kind here. Pale, dry *fino* is drunk not only as an apéritif but also with soup and fish courses. Rich dark *oloroso* goes particularly well after dinner. Brandy is another option as a *digestif*. Spanish brandy varies from excellent to rough: you usually get what you pay for. Other spirits are made under licence in Spain, and are usually cheap.

Hot Drinks

Coffee is typically served black *(solo)*, with a spot of milk *(cortado/tallat)*, or half and half with hot milk *(con leche/ amb llet)*. Orxata, made with ground tiger nuts and milk, is also popular, and is served both hot and cold.

Above from far left: paella; chocolates; lunch on the beach; tasty tapas.

Typical Menu Items in Catalan

Entrants/Primer Plat (Starter/First Course)

amanida green salad

arros negre black rice, squid and its ink

canelons a la barcelonina cannelloni stuffed with meat

cigrons chick-peas, often stewed with chard *(bledes),* spinach, tiny clams or cod

croquetes cassolanes homemade croquettes (with chicken, ham or salt cod)

empedrat white bean salad with tomatoes, onions, salt cod and olives

escudella thick soup with noodles, made from stock produced when boiling meat

espinacs a la catalana steamed spinach, lightly fried with raisins and pine nuts

faves a la catalana broad beans, stewed like lentils

gaspatxo Andalucian cold tomato soup

llenties lentils, usually with spicy sausage and black pudding

sopa de peix fish soup

verdures vegetable of the day, often overcooked with potatoes

Segon Plat (Main Course)

calamars a la romana/farcits squid fried in batter or stuffed

fetge liver

fricandó braised veal with wild mushrooms

mandonguilles meatballs

peix (lluç, tonyina, gambes, sèpia…) a la planxa fish (hake, tuna, prawns, cuttlefish) cooked on a griddle; meat (notably rabbit) is also cooked this way

pollastre rostit chicken roasted in a rich sauce

pollastre/carn arrebossada chicken/meat (usually beef) fried in breadcrumbs

salsitxes amb tomàquet thin sausages in tomato sauce

xai a la brasa lamb cooked on open wood or charcoal fire

Postre (Dessert)

flam crème caramel

fruite (poma, platan, pressec, sindria) fresh fruit (apple, banana, peach, watermelon)

gelat ice cream

macedonia fruit salad

mel i mató creamy curd cheese with honey

postre de music nuts and dried fruits, often served with moscatel (dessert wine)

pastis tart/cake

Below: cava and tapas for the masses.

SHOPPING

Barcelona is a great place to shop, from its innovative, designer-conscious showcases around the Passeig de Gràcia and Diagonal to the timeless independent shops in the Barri Gòtic and cutting-edge boutiques in El Born.

Shopping Hours
Most shops open between 9am and 10am and close for lunch between 1 and 2pm, opening again between 4 and 5pm until 8pm. Many clothes and food shops close at 8.30 or 9pm. The large department stores, chain stores and shopping galleries remain open through lunchtime. In the summer smaller shops may close on Saturday afternoon. Only bakeries, pastry shops and a few groceries are open on Sunday (until around 3pm).

In keeping with its reputation as a centre for style and design, Barcelona has an impressive range of fashion boutiques, antiques shops, state-of-the-art home interior stores and art galleries. Shopping is extremely pleasant here, as the city has not been totally overtaken by homogenous chain stores and still has many quirky and enticing family-owned shops. The best items to buy include trendy clothing, shoes and other leather products, antiques, books (Barcelona is the publishing capital of Spain), high-tech design and home furnishings.

SHOPPING AREAS

The Passeig de Gràcia, Rambla de Catalunya and interconnecting streets are good for chain stores, high-end fashions and boutiques. The same goes for the Barri Gòtic, which also has many artisanal shops, galleries and trendy souvenir sellers, plus hip clothes stores as you move towards El Born.

The Avinguda Diagonal, from the top of Rambla de Catalunya up to the roundabout that forms Plaça Francesc Macià, and the streets behind, are good for fashion at the top end of the market, while Gràcia is a relaxed, charming place to shop, with cutting-edge young designer fashion and jewellery.

DEPARTMENT STORES

The largest department store in Barcelona is El Corte Inglés, with a branch in Plaça de Catalunya, another in nearby Portal de l'Angel specialising in leisure, music, books and sports, and others in Avinguda Diagonal. All branches are open Monday to Saturday, from 10am till 10pm. The branches on the Plaça de Catalunya and Diagonal (no. 617) have excellent supermarkets.

FASHION

Designer Clothes

Toni Miró (no relation to the artist) is by far the most famous Catalan designer of mens- and womenswear, with clothes characterised by low-key design and clean lines. His shops, called Groc, are at Rambla de Catalunya 100, Carrer de Muntaner 385 and Carrer del Consell de Cent 349. Other designer names to look for include Adolfo Dominguez, David Valls and Jean Pierre Bua.

High-Street Fashion

In the old town, Carrer de la Portaferrissa and Portal de l'Angel are good for young fashion stores. On and around Carrer d'Avinyó there are a lot of trendy shops, such as Loft Avignon, and El Born is now a favourite spot for

boutiques. El Raval is catching up fast: Caníbal, on Carrer del Carmé 5, has fun, one-off designs, while Carrer de la Riera Baixa is lined with second-hand clothes boutiques.

Shoes

These are great value in Spain. Look out for Catalan and Spanish designers such as Yanko and Farrutx (Carrer del Roselló 218), which trade on sophisticated elegance. Lotusse (very well-made contemporary classics) and Camper (trendy, comfortable shoes) can be found at Tascón (branches in Passeig de Gràcia and El Born) or its own shops in Pelai, València, just off Passeig de Gràcia, and Elisabets in El Raval. The best areas for shoes and bags are Portal de l'Angel, Rambla de Catalunya, Passeig de Gràcia, Diagonal and the shopping malls.

FOOD

The best places to buy food are markets or *colmados* (corner grocer's shops).

Items to look out for include juicy olives freshly marinated in garlic, sausages (chorizo and *sobrasada*), ham (*jabugo* is the best), cheese (Manchego, Mahon, Idiazabal), nuts, dried fruit, handmade chocolates, *turrón* (a nougat-type delicacy, available in hard or soft form, eaten at Christmas), wine, cava and moscatel.

Some of the city's finest historic food stores include Casa Gispert (Carrer dels Sombrerers 23); Colmado Quilez (Rambla de Catalunya 63); chocolatiers Escribà (La Rambla 83); Fargas (Carrer dels Boters 2, on the corner of Pi and Cucurulla), for excellent *turrón*; and Xocoa (Carrer de Petritxol 11), another chocolatiers, whose innovative flavours include 'five peppers' and 'thyme'.

Múrria (Carrer de Roger de Llúria 85) is home to an exquisite range, including cava under their own label, in the prettiest of old Modernista interiors, while Planelles Donat (Portal de l'Angel 27) are specialists in *turrón* and do delicious ice cream in summer. The only hard thing is deciding which flavour to buy.

Above from far left: Màremagnum mall; interior design; Eixample fashions; Camper shoes.

Markets

There are covered markets, selling fruit, vegetables, meat and fish, in just about every *barrio*. Most open daily except Sunday from early morning until around 3pm. Try to go on days other than Monday, when the selection is poor because the central wholesale market does not open. The largest market is La Rambla's Boqueria, which opens till 8pm. The bargains are to be found in the maze of stalls at the back.

Below: historic hat shop in the Barri Gòtic.

MODERNISME

Architecture is on the agenda of many visitors to Barcelona, due mainly to the outlandish works of Antoni Gaudí and his Modernista contemporaries. The city's defining architectural style looked to the past for its main influences.

Tragic End
A reclusive figure in his later years, while he was working on the Sagrada Familia, Antoni Gaudí was run over by a tram in a street near to the church. The doctors were initially unable to identify the dishevelled old man who had been knocked over, thinking that he was a tramp. When it was finally discovered who he was, the entire city turned out for his funeral.

Modernisme is Barcelona's great contribution to architecture. Colourful and flamboyant, the architectural and artistic style emerged around the time of the Universal Exhibition, held in the Parc de la Ciutadella *(see p.58)*, in 1888 and continued until *c*.1930, thus corresponding to the Arts and Crafts and Art Nouveau (or Jugendstil, as it was known in Germany and Austria) movements in the rest of Europe. It shared with Arts and Crafts a focus on traditional styles and craftsmanship, and, with Art Nouveau, a preoccupation with sinuous lines and organic form and ornament and a rebellion against rigid designs and colourless stone and plaster.

Catalan Renaissance

In Barcelona the new style assumed nationalist motifs and significance, which may be why it has been carefully preserved. The movement was a part of the Catalan Renaixença (renaissance), which looked to the past, taking on Catalan Gothic and its tradition of iron work, as well as acknowledging the highly elaborate styles of Islamic Spain.

The city's 19th-century expansion (the Eixample) gave architects the freedom and space to experiment, and this area is where the majority of the city's Modernista buildings are located.

KEY FIGURES

The movement's greatest practitioners were Antoni Gaudí i Cornet (1852–1926), Lluís Domènech i Montaner (1850–1923), a professor of Barcelona University's School of Architecture, and one of his pupils, Josep Puig i Cadafalch (1867–1957). At the Universal Exhibition Domènech designed what is now the Museu Zoologia *(see p.59)*, based on Valencia's red-brick Gothic Stock Exchange, which afterwards became a workshop for ceramics, wrought iron and glass-making. Furnishings and details were an essential ingredient in Modernista buildings, in the same way that a coherent design was key to Arts and Crafts and Art Nouveau design.

In the years immediately following its heyday, Modernisme was considered to be the epitome of bad taste, but today the pendulum has swung back again, and Modernista buildings have become symbols of a vibrant city.

HIGHLIGHTS

Illa de la Discórdia

The best starting point to understand Modernisme is the 'block of discord', three neighbouring buildings in Passeig de Gràcia. The block gained its name because of the close juxtaposi-

tion of three outstanding buildings – Domènech's Casa Lléo Morera, Puig's Casa Amatller and Gaudí's Casa Batlló *(see p.67)* – each of which is in a conflicting style, although they are all categorised as Modernista.

Gaudí Buildings

Having worked under Josep Fontseré on the Parc de la Ciutadella and the Plaça del Rei *(see pp.34 and 38)*, Gaudí earned his first commission, the Casa Vicens *(see p.82)* in Gràcia, aged 32. In 1878 he met wealthy textile manufacturer Count Eusebi Güell, whose fortune and passion for experimental architecture – and his ability to accept the architect's wildly imaginative ideas – were crucial to Gaudí's rising star. It led to the building from 1886–8 of the Palau Güell *(see p.53)* and, later, from 1900, the Park Güell *(see p.71)*.

Gaudí's other key buildings include La Pedrera *(see p.68)*, on which he worked from 1905, Casa Batlló *(see above)* and the monumental Sagrada Família *(see p.70)*, on which he travailed from 1883; the deeply religious architect was still designing the church, with its extravagant organic lines, when he died aged 74 in 1926 *(see left)*.

Other Key Works

Other key Modernista works include the Unesco-protected Palau de la Música Catalana *(see p.44)*, an extraordinarily sumptuous building, with a spectacular interior. Its facade, crowded with sculptures and dazzling mosaics, is rather cramped down Carrer de Sant Francesc de Paula. There are tours of the building, but it is best if you can attend a concert beneath the stained-glass dome that suffuses the auditorium with a mellow light.

Hospital de la Santa Creu i de Sant Pau *(see p.71)*, designed by Domènech, was the most advanced in Europe when it was completed in 1901. It is essentially a series of pavilions connected by underground tunnels and is one of the Modernista highlights of the city.

Also by Domènech, at Carrer de Mallorca 291, is Casa Thomas, built for the engraving business of a relative. It now houses b.d., an upmarket design shop that sells excellent reproductions of Modernista furniture and fittings and is worth a visit.

Key works by Puig i Cadafalch include the Casaramona textile factory, built at the foot of Montjuïc *(see p.73)* and now the vibrant CaixaForum cultural centre *(see p.75)*.

Above from far left: Hospital de la Santa Creu i de Sant Pau; Palau de la Música Catalana; stained glass at the Casa Batlló; ironwork detail on the Palau Güell.

St George and the Dragon
Catalonia's patron saint was a favourite theme of the Modernistas. Gaudí's Casa Batlló is dedicated to the saint, with spiny dragons' 'bones' for window frames.

Below: organic bench, decorated with colourful Modernista *trencadis* (mosaic made from broken tiles) in Gaudí's Park Güell.

CATALAN

Visitors will quickly become aware that Catalan is the official language of Barcelona and Catalonia. Not only are all signs in Catalan, but Catalan is spoken among Barcelonans, even in a group of non-Catalan speakers.

Catalan is a Romance language, meaning it is Latin based, a sister to Castilian (Spanish), French, Italian and Portuguese. It has a staccato quality that makes it sound very different from Castilian, though when written its similarities are more apparent.

EARLY USE

Catalan began to be used widely from the 13th century, particularly in legal codes, such as the *Consolat de Mar*, which laid down laws governing Mediterranean shipping. The four Great Chronicles describing the life of Jaume I (the Conqueror) are also from this time. One of the families who ended up in Mallorca as a result of Jaume's conquests was that of Ramón Lull (1232–1315), whose religious and philosophic writings in Catalan (as well as Latin and Arabic) were prodigious.

GOLDEN AGE

The Golden Age of Catalan literature was in the 15th century, when Jocs Florals (floral games) were introduced as linguistic competitions for troubadors. This was in imitation of similar events in Toulouse in France, where Languedocian, a regional language similar to Catalan, was spoken. *Tirant lo Blanc*, a

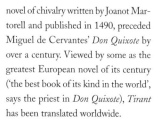

novel of chivalry written by Joanot Martorell and published in 1490, preceded Miguel de Cervantes' *Don Quixote* by over a century. Viewed by some as the greatest European novel of its century ('the best book of its kind in the world', says the priest in *Don Quixote*), *Tirant* has been translated worldwide.

18TH CENTURY

After the War of Succession (1705–15), Catalonia was punished for siding with the Habsburg Archduke Charles. Castilian became the official language, and Catalan was relegated to religious and popular use. It was not until the industrial revolution, and the emergence of a dynamic middle class during the 19th century, that an economic and cultural revival known as the Renaixença (Renaissance) enabled Catalan to recover as a vehicle of culture.

Its leading lights were poets, notably Jacint Verdaguer (1845–1902), a priest, who won many prizes in the revived Jocs Florals. His poetry is still required reading in schools, and his hymn *El Virolai* is sung daily by the choir in Montserrat. The Catalan nationalist sentiment informed all the arts; Modernisme architecture, which harked back to the Golden Age, can be said to be a showpiece of Catalan aspiration.

Usage
Catalan is spoken by at least six million people in Catalonia, Valencia, the Roussillon region of France, Andorra and some border areas of Aragón. It is also spoken in the Balearic Islands and the city of Alghero in Sardinia, both of which were ruled by Catalonia in the 13th to 14th centuries.

20TH CENTURY

In 1907 the Institut d'Estudis Catalans was formed for 'the re-establishment and organisation of all things relating to Catalan culture'. When the Generalitat was set up in 1931, Catalan again enjoyed the status of official language.

However, Franco's victory in the Spanish Civil War (1936–9) stamped out Catalan. It was banned entirely from public use, as were Galician and Basque, the other regional languages of Spain. Books, newspapers and films were subjected to draconian censorship. The enforced implementation of an all-Castilian education system meant that a generation of Catalan speakers were unable to read or write their mother tongue, which they continued to use.

OFFICAL LANGUAGE

With the recovery of democracy in Spain, Catalan was established alongside Castilian as the official language of Catalonia. Campaigns were launched, and staunch nationalists made their views felt. It was not an easy time: many people in the city are not native Catalans and were worried that their children would be taught in a language they did not understand. But the government set about implementing a policy of 'linguistic normalisation', whereby Catalan was reinstated in all aspects of public life, government and the media. In 1990 the European Parliament passed a resolution recognising Catalan and its use in the European Union, and there was even a move to send a separate Catalan national team to the 1992 Olympics.

Nowdays, Catalan thrives in the arts and sciences, the media and advertising. Barcelona is a bilingual city, although varying degrees of proficiency in its different languages are evident. Some older people, educated before the Civil War, may have an imperfect knowledge of Castilian, and, while Catalan is almost universally understood, older immigrants from elsewhere in Spain may not speak it. People schooled during the past two decades are generally proficient in both languages.

The rationale behind the linguistic policy is that if Catalan is not actively defended it will decay into a local *patois*. Its detractors, meanwhile, allege narrow-minded nationalism, but the vociferous nationalism that came with autonomy has now mellowed and for the most part the two languages happily co-exist.

Above from far left: signs in Catalan.

Shops/Museums
Open *Obert*
Closed *Tancat*
Monday *Dilluns*
Tuesday *Dimarts*
Wednesday
   Mimecres
Thursday *Dijous*
Friday *Divendres*
Satyrday *Dissabetes*
Sunday *Diumenge*

Useful Phrases

Good morning *Bon dia*

Good afternoon/evening *Bona tarda*

Good night *Bona nit*

How are you? *Com està vostè?*

Very well thank you, and you? *Molt bé, gràcies i vostè?*

Goodbye, see you again *Adéu, a reveure*

See you later *Fins després*

See you tomorrow *Fins demà*

What's your name? *Com us diu?*

My name is … *Em dic …*

1–10: *U/un/una, dos/dues, tres, quatre, cinc, sis, set, vuit, nou, deu*

HISTORY: KEY DATES

The city rose to power under Catalonia's medieval count-kings, then fell into decline and subject to the control of Madrid. The urge to break out of this inertia, and a deep Catalan identity, are key to Barcelona's inventive energy.

Did You Know?
In 1836, the first steamship rolled off a slipway in Barceloneta; gaslight was introduced in 1842; and in 1848 Spain's first railway linked Barcelona to Mataró, some 30km (19 miles) north.

Ramón Casas
Casas (1866–1932) was one of the most representative of the Modernista artists who flourished in the late 19th century in Barcelona. Above are his self-portrait on a tandem, painted for the café El Quatre Gats, *(see pp.35 and 123)* and a portrait of a woman.

EARLY HISTORY TO THE GOLDEN AGE

237 BC	The Carthaginian Hamilcar Barca makes a base at Barcino.
206 BC	The Romans defeat the Carthaginians.
AD 531–54	Barcelona is made capital of the Visigoths.
711	Moorish invasion of Spain; they remain until 1492.
878	Wilfred (Guifré) the Hairy founds dynasty of counts of Barcelona.
1096–1131	Ramón Berenguer III extends the Catalan empire.
1213–76	Jaume I consolidates the empire, and expands Barcelona.
1359	The Corts Catalanes (Parliament of Catalonia) is established. The 14th century is the Golden Age of Catalonia.
1395	The Jocs Florals – annual competitions for poets and troubadors – are initiated in Catalonia.

IMPERIAL SPAIN

1469	Ferdinand and Isabella unite Aragón and Castile.
1494	The administration of Catalonia is put under Castilian control.
1516	Carlos I (Charles V, Holy Roman Emperor) takes the throne.
1659	Catalan territories north of the Pyrenees are ceded to France.
1701–13	War of Spanish Succession.
1713–14	Siege of Barcelona by Felipe V's forces; Ciutadella fortress built.
1835	Convents are disbanded by government decree; many are pulled down to give way to such new buildings as the Liceu, Boqueria and Palau de la Música Catalana.
1860	The building of the Eixample, designed by Ildefons Cerdà, begins.
1883	Antoni Gaudí begins work on the Sagrada Família.

THE MODERN ERA

1888	Barcelona hosts its first Universal Exhibition.
1897	The café Els Quatre Gats opens and becomes haunt of artists and writers. Picasso, aged 19, exhibits here for the first time.

1914	The Mancomunitat (provincial government) is formed in Catalonia.
1923	General Primo de Rivera sets up dictatorship and bans Catalan.
1929	A second Universal Exhibition is held, in the grounds of Montjuïc. Buildings including the Poble Espanyol are constructed.
1931	The Republican party comes to power.
1932	Catalonia is granted a short-lived statute of independence.
1936–9	Civil War ends in Franco's rule and isolates Spain. The Catalan language and the expression of Catalan customs are banned.
1975	Franco dies, and Juan Carlos is made king. Catalan is recognised as an official language.
1979	Statute of Autonomy; Catalan is restored as an official language.
1980	Jordi Pujol becomes president of Catalonia.
1986	Spain joins European Community (European Union). A wave of building, which is presided over by socialist mayor Pasqual Maragall (a trained town planner), begins in preparation for the Olympics.
1992	The Olympic Games are held in Barcelona.
1994	The Liceu opera house is devastated by fire.

21ST CENTURY

2003	Pujol is replaced as president of Catalonia by Pasqual Maragall.
2004	The city extends north, around Diagonal Mar, for Forum 2004. The city council becomes the first in Spain to oppose bullfighting.
2006	A new Catalan statute is passed. Jordi Hereu becomes the third socialist mayor of the city. Maragall stands down, and is replaced by José Montilla as president.

Above from far left: depiction of 13th-century *Assault on the City of Mallorca*, in the Palau Nacional; Barcelona falls to the armies of Felipe V, 11 September 1714.

Commemorations and Celebrations
The year 1992 was not just an important date for Barcelona because of the Olympics. It was also the 500th anniversary of Columbus's discovery of America and the expulsion of the Moors from Spain. It was not in fact until 1493 that Columbus – Cristobal Colom – returned in triumph to Barcelona, to be received by Ferdinand and Isabella in the Saló de Tinell in the Royal Palace. The Genoese navigator, whose statue stands on a great plinth at the foot of La Rambla, did Barcelona little good with his discovery. Seville was the city granted the right to trade with the New World, and Barcelona suffered economic decline.

Left: poster advertising the Barcelona Universal Exhibition in 1929.

WALKS AND TOURS

LA RAMBLA

One of the world's most attractive avenues, La Rambla is the first place any visitor to Barcelona should head for. Animated day and night, it always has something worth seeing – even if it is just the passers-by.

> **DISTANCE** 1.5km (1 mile)
> **TIME** 1½ hours
> **START** Plaça de Catalunya
> **END** Port Vell
> **POINTS TO NOTE**
> This is an easy stroll that can be done at any time of day. Unfortunately, you should be on your guard against pick-pockets on this popular stretch.

Below: bird's eye view of the Rambla.

This leafy pedestrian avenue was once a river running beside the old city wall to the sea. On the left as you head down to the port is the Ciutat Vella, the Old Town, with tempting lanes and alleys *(see pp.34 and 40)*, while signs to the modern Museu de Art Contemporanea (MACBA) and Casa Güell, the only Gaudí building in this area, beckon on the right (south-west), in the old working-class Raval district *(see p.50)*. Traffic rumbles over the cobbles either side of the wide, plane-tree shaded promenade, and you will cross back and forth, as sights and attractions entice.

PLAÇA DE CATALUNYA

At the top of La Rambla is the **Plaça de Catalunya ❶**, where the Old Town ends and the new city (the Eixample, *see p.66*), laid out during the early 20th century and extending inland, begins. A pavement star in the middle of this large open square marks the geographical heart of the city.

The 1925 El Corte Inglés ('The English Style') department store is on the north-east side of the square. The airport bus stops beside it, and nearby is the 'i' sign of the underground **tourist information** centre. An angular monument by local sculptor Josep María Subirachs commemorates Fran-

cesc Macià (1859–1933), President of the Generalitat before the Civil War. Chess players tend to gather nearby. Flanking the square to the southwest is the popular **Café Zurich,** see ⑪①.

LA RAMBLA

From here the **Rambla** (from the verb 'ramblar', meaning to stroll) begins, a 1.5-km (1-mile) promenade of colourful stalls selling such items as birds, flowers, newspapers and magazines, with pavement cafés sheltered beneath its established plane trees. Musicians, mime artists, tango dancers, fire eaters, fortune tellers and other entertainers add to the diversion day and night.

A fashionable place to stroll since the 19th century, La Rambla is in fact made up of five different *rambles*: Canaletes, Estudis, Sant Josep, Caputxins and Santa Mònica, the last three taking their names from convents that lined the south-west (right-hand) side of the street, giving it the name of 'Convent Way'. In the 1830s these powerful institutions were

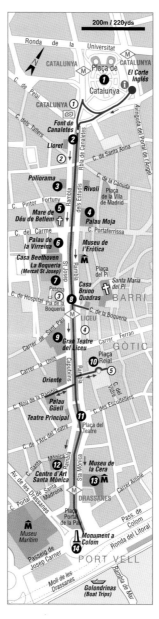

Food and Drink 🍴
① CAFÉ ZURICH
Plaça de Catalunya; tel: 93 317 91 52; €
This city institution was rebuilt as part of El Triangle commercial centre, when the city was propelled into the 20th century for the 1992 Olympic Games. Slow down at its pavement tables, which spill onto the square, and choose from café standards of sandwiches, salads, etc, plus delicious pastries and coffee.

Above from far left: El Corte Inglés; statue on the Plaça de Catalunya; perfume bottles in the Triangle shopping centre; mid-19th-century ironwork on the Rambla.

Above: flowers, street performer and fresh fruit on the Rambla.

Underground Hub
Plaça de Catalunya is the city's main transport hub, with a warren of underground passages leading to both FGC trains (for the suburbs) and national Renfe trains; three metro lines also stop here.

City Gates
The four city gates that gave access into the Old Town from La Rambla were at Santa Ana, La Boqueria, Porta- ferrissa and Drassanes. An attractive tiled fountain *(illustrated above)* in Carrer de la Porta- ferrissa shows how they once looked.

Below: Casa Beethoven's *raison d'être* in lights.

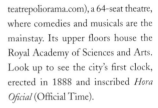

reduced by riots and reforms. Until the 15th century, the city wall ran down the south-western side of the avenue.

Top of the Avenue
The first section, **Rambla de Canaletes**, takes its name from the 19th-century drinking fountain **Font de Canaletes** ❷, now a popular meeting place. Jubi- lant Barça fans, of all ages, traditionally gather here to celebrate their team's vic- tories. The story goes that if you drink from the fountain's waters, you are sure to return to Barcelona. If, however, you would prefer a taste of something less puritanical, make a brief detour left into Carrer dels Tallers, for **Boadas**, see ❶❷.

Back on the main drag, the next stretch is the **Rambla dels Estudis**, named after the university that was here until 1714. At no. 115, on the right, is **Poliorama** ❸ (tel: 93 317 75 99; www.

Food and Drink 🍴
② BOADAS
Carrer dels Tallers 1; tel: 93 318 88 26; €
The oldest cocktail bar in town and arguably the most atmos- pheric, with its 1930s decor and walls lined with caricatures of the original owner, after whom the bar is named. He mixed a mean *mojito*, a skill learned from his Cuban parents, and his daughter, Dolors Boadas, continues the tradition.

③ PASTILERIA ESCRIBÀ
Rambla de les Flores 83; tel: 93 301 60 27; €
This café is just one outlet of the famous Escribà patisserie and chocolate makers, with fare as enchanting as its façade.

teatrepoliorama.com), a 64-seat theatre, where comedies and musicals are the mainstay. Its upper floors house the Royal Academy of Sciences and Arts. Look up to see the city's first clock, erected in 1888 and inscribed *Hora Oficial* (Official Time).

Palau Moja
Opposite, beyond the Hotel Rivoli, is the colonnade of the bookshop of the Generalitat (Catalonia's autonomous government), which has maps and lavish books on the city and region. The shop occupies part of the ground floor of the 18th-century, neoclassical **Palau Moja** ❹ (Carrer de la Portaferrissa 1; tel: 93 316 27 40, call ahead to arrange a visit; free), belonging to the Generalitat's Department of Culture. Hosting tem- porary exhibitions, the building is worth dipping into just to see the fine first- floor Grand Salon's Baroque murals by Francesc Pla (1743–92). The main entrance to the palace, as well as the entrance to the palace courtyard, is in Carrer de la Portaferrissa, a lively shop- ping street that was one of the main alleys into the Old Town. Today the street is popular with shoppers for its shoes, fashion and leather goods.

Mare de Deu de Betlem
Opposite the palace across La Rambla is the **Mare de Déu de Betlem** ❺ (Carrer del Carme 2; tel: 93 318 38 23; free), a 17th-century Baroque church, bare since being burnt out in the Civil War and only recently renovated. This was part of a Jesuit convent, and a statue of the order's founder, the Basque-born

saint, Ignatius Loyola, is joined by St Boromeu to flank the entrance.

Palau de la Virreina

Beyond the church, the pavement is set back to give a grander vista of the **Palau de la Virreina ⑥** (La Rambla 99; tel: 93 316 10 00; www.bcn.es; Tue–Sat 11am–2pm, 4–8pm, Sun 11am–3pm; charge), an imposing Rococo building with lavish masonry and metalwork decoration. It was completed in 1777 for Manuel Amat, Spain's pleasure-loving viceroy to Peru, but he died shortly after taking up residence.

Built around two courtyards, it is now a venue for major exhibitions. One courtyard is used to display the city's impressive carnival 'giants', huge figures that are paraded through the streets during traditional celebrations. At the front of the building is a box office for events in the city.

Beside the palace is the dinky Modernista **Casa Beethoven** *(see left)*, which has been selling sheet music since 1920. On the other side of the street, at no. 96, the first-floor **Museu de l'Eròtica** (tel: 93 318 98 65; www.erotica-museum.com; daily 10am–2am; charge) show-cases saucy artworks, photographs and sculptures, etc.

La Boqueria

The 19th-century Mercat de Sant Josep, better known as **La Boqueria ⑦** (Mon–Sat 7am–8pm), is named after the convent that stood just past the Palau de la Virreina. Here, top restau-rateurs and other gourmets do their early-morning shopping. Look out for fungi in season, super-fresh vegeta-bles and fruit, delectable ranges of olives, cheeses and nuts, butchers' stalls selling all you need for nose-to-tail eating, plus seafood glistening on ice.

Just beyond the market on the corner of Carrer Petxina is an attractive mosaic-fronted Modernista shop, the **Antigua Casa Figueras**. It now houses the **Pastileria Escribà**, see ⑪③, owned by the Barcelona chocolate-producing dynasty, the Escribà family.

Pla de la Boqueria

In front of the market is the square of the same name, **Pla de la Boqueria ⑧**.

Above from far left: Miró's pavement by Pla de la Boqueria; market sign; Boqueria stained glass; market-fresh fish.

Breakfast at La Boqueria

The market is a great place to eat at any time of the day, but for a special experience come early and fill up with an *esmorçar de cullera*, a hearty breakfast, in one of its bars. The 18-seater Quim de la Boqueria is where local foodies gather from 8am for break-fast prepared by Quim Márquez, whose innovative dishes include *fricassée* of artichokes and white asparagus, lamb strips cooked in dark beer, and tiny clams steamed in sparkling wine. Pinotxo, open from 6am, is a lively market bar specialising in oysters and cava, and there is always a warm welcome here from the Bayen family. Alternatively, try the equally busy Kiosk Universal.

At the point where it breaks up the line of trees, lanes on the left lead into the Barri Gòtic *(see p.34)*. When the old city walls were in place, Pla de la Boqueria was the place of public executions. Nowadays, it is a considerably more pleasant place, enlivened by a colourful mosaic pavement by Joan Miró.

Beside it is **Casa Bruno Quadras**, built in the Oriental style, decorated with fans, lanterns and an elaborate coiling green Chinese dragon by Josep Vilaseca. It was originally designed to house an umbrella shop in the mid-1880s, but now shelters a savings bank.

Gran Teatre del Liceu

The block from Carrer de Sant Pau to Carrer de la Unió is taken up by the **Gran Teatre del Liceu** 9 (bookings tel: 902 53 33 53; www.liceubarcelona.com; tours daily 10am–1pm; charge). The limited facilities inside this classic,

plush 19th-century opera house were improved when the building was reconstructed following a major fire in 1994. One of the city's great institutions, it attracts world-renowned opera stars and also hosts jazz, cabaret and film (including some free entertainment in the foyer). There is a shop and café in the basement, though the historic **Café de l'Opera**, see ⑪④, opened in 1929 and one of the few remaining traditional cafés in the city, is just on the other side of La Rambla.

Vintage Hotels

Many historic hotels line La Rambla. Among them is the **Oriente** *(see p.114)*, just beyond the Liceu. The interior cloister of the Franciscan College of St Bonaventura, on which the latter hotel was built, remains intact.

The first turning on the right after the Oriente is **Carrer Nou de la Rambla**, housing, just along on the left, at nos 3–5, **Palau Güell** *(see p.53)*, the only building by Gaudí in the Old Town.

Plaça Reial

Opposite Carrer Nou de la Rambla, a faded grand arch leads into the **Plaça Reial** ⑩, one of the city's liveliest squares. Beneath its colonnades are cafés such as **El Taxidermista**, see ⑪⑤. At no. 17 is legendary jazz club, **Jamboree** (tel: 93 319 17 89; www.masimas.com; daily 8pm–11am; charge), which has been entertaining people since the 1960s. Top jazz musicians perform in its intimate vaulted basement and it also hosts club nights and Latin, funk, soul and hip-hop acts.

Towards the Port

After the Plaça Reial, the Rambla opens up on the left into **Plaça del Teatre** ⓫, where portrait artists ply their trade and old men typically sit for hours over coffee in Cosmos, a traditional café-restaurant. Barcelona's first theatre was on this site, and Frederic Soler (1835–95), founder of its present incarnation, the **Teatre Principal**, is commemorated in an imposing statue. He is unfortunately best remembered these days because a public toilet has been built beneath the statue – a great relief (literally), since bars are increasingly unwelcoming to non-clients using their facilities.

Further down, at La Rambla 7, on the right, is the **Centre d'Art Santa Mònica** ⓬ (tel: 93 316 28 10; www. centredartsantamonica.net; Tue–Sat 11am–8pm, Sun 11am–3pm; free). The former cloisters have been converted into three storeys of open gallery space, mostly for art installations. The second-floor bar and café have a substantial terrace with views over the Rambla. A cultural information centre is on the ground floor.

The old-fashioned green ticket booth in the middle of La Rambla at this point sells tickets for the **Museu de la Cera** ⓭ (Wax Museum; Passatge de la Banca; tel: 93 317 26 49; www. museoceraben.com; winter: Mon–Fri 10am–1.30pm, 4–7.30pm, Sat–Sun 11am–2pm, 4.30–8.30pm; summer: 10am–10pm; charge). More than 360 waxworks of mainly Spanish personalities appear in this handsome former bank. Inside is also El Bosc de les Fades, an enchanted 'forest' with magically lit gnarled trees and gnomes.

Monument a Colom

You can't miss the final stop on this tour, the 50-m (165-ft) high **Monument a Colom** ⓮ (Columbus Monument; tel: 93 302 52 24; daily 10am–6.30pm; charge), designed by Gaietà Buïgas, with a crowning sculpture of Columbus by Rafael Arché, for the Universal Exhibition of 1888. Note that Columbus is not pointing towards the New World, as intended; locals claim that he is simply pointing to the sea. For a great view of the port and the city, take the elevator to the top.

Just south of the statue is the seafront and **Port Vell**, where the Rambla turns into the **Rambla de Mar** *(see p.54)*, a walkway over to the marina.

Above from far left: inside the Liceu opera house; José Carreras and Montserrat Caballe; shopping on the Rambla; Oriental dragon and fan on the Casa Bruno Quadras.

Pipa Club

From 6pm daily smokers can enjoy unrestricted puffs at the Pipa Club (Plaça Reial 3; tel: 93 302 47 32; www.bpipa club.com). It has a number of rooms and a Victorian, clubby atmosphere, and serves food. It also puts on occasional live jazz.

Below: city bikes by the port.

ROYAL BARRI GÒTIC

The complex comprising the cathedral and royal palace is at the heart of the Old Town, which also incorporates a chunk of Roman Barcino. These imposing constructions contrast with the area's delicate cloisters and narrow lanes.

Above: palm trees and lamp-posts by Gaudí, the architect's first public work, in the Plaça del Rei.

DISTANCE 1.5km (1 mile)
TIME 3–4 hours
START Avinguda del Portal de l'Angel
END Plaça del Rei
POINTS TO NOTE

This is an easy stroll through the pedestrianised streets of one of the most complete medieval quarters in Europe. Note that these lanes tend to be very busy on Saturdays.

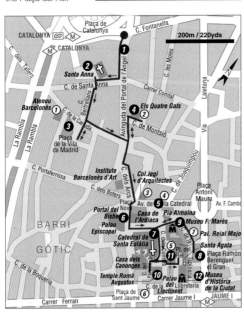

This walk starts at the bottom of Plaça de Catalunya, once the location of the Portal de l'Angel, the main inland gate into the medieval city. It can be combined with elements of the following walk, covering the 'Official Barri Gòtic', *(see p.40).*

AVINGUDA DEL PORTAL DE L'ANGEL

The busy **Avinguda del Portal de l'Angel ❶** leads into the Barri Gòtic from the Plaça de Catalunya. This wide shopping thoroughfare is ideal if you are hunting for shoes or moderately priced fashion.

Santa Anna

An early diversion awaits in the first turning on the right, **Carrer de Santa Anna**. Iron gates half-way down on the right, by a flower stall, lead to the two-tiered Gothic cloisters of the medieval church of **Santa Anna ❷** (Mon–Sat 9am–1pm, 6.30–8pm; feast days 10am–2pm; free). Built for the Knights Templar in the 12th century, the church's cloister and chapter house are still intact.

The Necropolis

From Santa Anna go down Carrer de Bertrellans, opposite the wonderful fan shop Guantería Alonso, into **Plaça de**

la Vila de Madrid ❸, which has been modelled to show off a Roman necropolis, discovered in the 1950s. This, however, is rather overpowered by the large Decathlon sports store, which dominates the square.

Opposite, at Carrer de la Canuda 6, is a palatial 18th-century mansion that in 1860 became home to the **Ateneu Barcelonès** cultural centre. Inside are fine paintings by Francesc Pla and, at the back, an attractive garden. Still a cultural centre, it holds temporary exhibitions and also has a good restaurant, **Ateneu**, see ⑪①.

Els Quatre Gats

Now return to Avinguda del Portal de l'Angel and just back up the street on the far side is Carrer de Montsió, where tucked away is Casa Martí, a fine Modernista building designed in 1897 by architect Puig i Cadafalch. It became famous as **Els Quatre Gats** ❹ (The Four Cats), see ⑪②, an arty café frequented by Barcelona's artists around the start of the 20th century.

Art Colleges

Continue down Avinguda del Portal de l'Angel, taking the left fork past the **Institute Barcelonès d'Art**, home of the Reial Cercle Artístic, which has a restaurant and exhibition space.

Beyond it on the left is the **Col.legi d'Arquitectes**, the front of which is surmounted by a frieze designed by Picasso and executed by the Norwegian artist Carl Nesjar. Reminiscent of cave drawings and completed in 1961, it was Picasso's first work to

appear in Spain since his self-imposed exile after the Civil War. The college has a pleasant restaurant, see ⑪③.

ROMAN GATES

The lane now opens out on to **Avinguda de la Catedral** ❺. The Roman wall that encircled the 4th-century city begins its surviving 1.5-km (1-mile) stretch here. The wall, constructed using colossal stones, the largest of which is some 3.5-m (12-ft) thick and 9.5-m (30-ft) high, originally had 78 square towers, of which several remain.

One tower forms the **Portal del Bisbe** ❻, beside which you can see remains of the aqueduct that brought

Above from far left: the area's atmospheric alleyways; the Casa de l'Ardiaca (see p.36).

Brilliant Barcelona At the end of the 16th century, writer Lope de Vegas wrote, 'Just as a splendid façade enhances the value of a building, so great Barcelona stands at the entrance to Spain, like a portico framing a famous threshold.'

Below: details of Picasso's frieze (executed by Carl Nesjar) above the Col.legi d'Arquitectes.

Food and Drink 🍴

① ATENEU
Carrer de la Canuda 6; tel: 93 318 52 38; €€
The restaurant in Ateneu Barcelonès cultural centre, beside Plaça de la Vila de Madrid, cooks up hearty Catalan farmyard favourites including duck, goose and rabbit.

② ELS QUATRE GATS
Carrer de Montsió 3; tel: 93 317 30 22; €€
In this historic arts café and restaurant, 19-year-old Pablo Picasso had his first exhibition in 1900. Risk being a tourist for the sake of eating here: the food is very acceptable and the sense of place a big pull.

③ COL.LEGI D'ARQUITECTES
Plaça Nova 5; tel: 93 306 78 50; closed weekends; €
The cafeteria on the ground floor of the architects' college does innovative fare and a great-value lunch menu.

Rooftop View

For a good view of the Barri Gòtic and a close-up of the spires, take the elevator from the nave (to the left of the entrance) to the roof of the cathedral. It is well worth the couple of euros for the view.

Above: the famously bad-tempered cathedral geese.

water to the Roman city. Through this 'gate' on the right is the **Palau Episcopal** (Bishops' Palace; tel: 93 301 10 84), built in 1769 around the 12th-century courtyard, which is visible through the main entrance.

The interiors of three other Roman towers can be seen in the **Casa de l'Ardiaca** (Archdeacon's House; tel: 93 318 11 95; free), next to the cathedral at Carrer de Santa Llúcia 1. The house has an attractive patio, in which a palm tree towers over a fountain. Note here the letterbox decorated with swallows and tortoises – signifying swift and slow mail – added in 1908 by Modernista architect Domènech i Montaner.

Facing the Casa de l'Ardiaca is the atmospheric Romanesque chapel of **Santa Eulàlia**, built in 1269 and one of the earliest parts of the cathedral, which it adjoins.

CATEDRAL DE SANTA EULÀLIA

There has been a Christian church on Plaça de la Seu, the site of the present cathedral, since the 10th century. The first was destroyed by Al-Mansur, vizier of Córdoba, in AD 985. The current **Catedral de Santa Eulàlia ⓐ** (tel: 93 342 82 60; www.catedralbcn.org; Mon–Fri 8am–12.45pm, 5–7.30pm, Sat 8am–12.45pm, 5–6pm, Sun 8–9am, 5–6pm; cloister daily 9am–12.30pm, 5–7pm; free) was begun in 1298 under Jaume II and completed in 1417, though its main, west façade was not finished until the early 20th century.

Cathedral Interior

The austere, lofty cathedral has three naves and a central choir. Below the altar is the crypt of St Eulàlia, whose remains

Sunday Sardana

Every Sunday morning people gather outside the cathedral to dance Catalonia's traditional *sardana*. When the music starts, friends hold hands to form circles, placing any bags they are carrying in the centre of the ring. Anyone can join in simply by slipping in between two people – though not between a man and the woman on his right. When the circles grow too large, breakaway groups form new ones. The serious looks on the dancers' faces are the result of having to keep count of the short, sedate, steps and the bouncy long ones, so that everyone finishes exactly on cue. The accompanying band or *cobla*, has 11 players, and the leader, seated, plays a *flabiol* (three-holed flute) and taps the rhythm on a *tabal* strapped to his arm. Each tune lasts about 10 minutes and in an *audació*, a normal performance, there will be half a dozen tunes. The origins of the music date from the mid-19th century.

were placed here 1,000 years after she was martyred in the Roman purges of Dacian; her alabaster tomb, behind the altar, was carved in 1327. Of the 29 side chapels, the most notable is that of St Salvador, which features a *Transfiguration* (1442) by Bernat Martorell.

A plaque in the baptistery, to the left of the entrance, notes that the first six Carib Indians brought to Europe by Columbus were baptised here on 1 April 1493. In the Chapel of Christ Lepanto, to the right of the entrance, you can see the crucifix borne in battle by the Christian flagship in the decisive Battle of Lepanto in 1571, which routed the North Africans from the high seas.

Cloisters

Among the cathedral's highlights are its cloisters, which are enclosed by a 15th-century iron railing. The cool ambience is emphasised by the mossy Font de les Oques, a drinking fountain that takes its name from the 13 geese (one for every year that St Eulàlia lived) that reside here. Note on the floor the faint engraving of shoes and scissors reflecting the various guilds (of cobblers and tailors, etc.) that paid for the chapel.

Around the Cathedral

Opposite the cathedral is the **Hotel Colon**, see ⑪④. On the far side of the square, the Roman wall continues past the 15th-century almshouse, **Pia Almoina**, housing the **Museu Diocesa** (Avinguda de la Catedral 4; tel: 93 315 22 13; Tue–Sat 10am–2pm, Sun 11am–2pm; charge), showcasing altarpieces, religious sculpture and other icons.

The wall then runs down Carrer de la Tapineria to **Plaça de Ramón Berenguer el Gran ❽**. The equestrian statue here, of the 12th-century count, who added the French region of Provence to Catalonia by marriage, is by Josep Llimona (1864–1934).

MUSEU
FREDERIC MARÈS

To the left of the cathedral, Carrer dels Comtes leads down beside the complex of the former royal palace of the count-kings of Barcelona-Aragón. On the left, at Plaça de Sant Iu 5–6, is the **Museu Frederic Marès ❾** (tel: 93 319 58 00; www.museumares.bcn.es; Tue–Sat 10am–7pm, Sun 10am–3pm; charge except Wed 3–7pm). In the 13th century this was the bishop's palace, before becoming home to the counts of Barcelona and the count-kings of Barcelona-Aragón.

It now houses an extraordinary collection of mainly religious artefacts brought together by Marès, a wealthy local sculptor who lived in the building and had a studio here until his death, at the age of 97, in 1991. There is a large

Above from far left: view from the cathedral roof; cathedral candles *(left)*, façade *(middle)* and lofty interior *(right)*.

Bargain Hunting
Every Thursday there is an antiques and bric-à-brac market in Plaça Nova outside the cathedral.

Above from left: stonework *(left)*, tiles *(middle)* and icon *(right)* in the Museu Frederic Marès; Plaça del Rei.

Romanesque collection, with some particularly fine crucifixes, and even entire portals.

On the upper floors is a delightful hotchpotch of memorabilia, including toys, pipes, locks, clocks, cameras and postcards, and Marès's study and studio. Sheltered in the courtyard is a nice café, see ⑪⑤.

TEMPLE ROMÀ D'AUGUSTI

For a slight detour, follow the cathedral's curving walls around Carrer de la Pietat, beside the 14th- to 16th-century **Casa dels Canonges**, and take the first left, Carrer del Paradis. Step inside the entrance of no. 7 to see four Corinthian columns that were part of the **Temple Romà d'Augusti** ❿ (Temple of Augustus; tel: 93 315 11 11; Tue–Sat 10am–8pm; free). Set on the highest point in the oppidum, this was the main religious building here in Roman times and is now the city's largest single relic from that period.

PALAU DEL LLOCTINENT

Back by the Museu Frederic Marès – or, rather, just beyond – a handsome doorway leads into the elegant courtyard of the **Palau del Lloctinent** ⓫ (currently undergoing restoration), which takes its name from the Lloctinent (lord lieutenant – in this case, viceroy), who resided here. Part of the former royal palace (Palau Reial), and designed in the Renaissance style between 1549 and 1557 by architect Antoni Carbonell, the building was later embellished in the Catalan Gothic style – the latter is typified by horizontal lines and solid, plain walls (rather than lofty spaces, as in classic Gothic) between columns, octagonal towers and flat roofs.

In addition to housing the viceroy, the building also sheltered the archive of the Crown of Aragón and, on a darker note, was the headquarters of the Spanish Inquisition in Barcelona.

PLAÇA DEL REI

Adjacent is the **Plaça del Rei**, the heart of the old royal city.

Museu d'Història de la Ciutat
The main royal buildings around the square are accessed through the excellent **Museu d'Història de la Ciutat** ⓬ (City History Museum; Plaça del Rei 1; tel: 93 315 11 11; www.museuhistoria.bcn.es; Oct–May: Tue–Sat 10am–2pm, 4–8pm, Sun 10am–3pm, June–Sept: Tue–Sat 10am–8pm, Sun 10am–3pm; charge includes

Below: Museu d'Història de la Ciutat.

admission to the former royal palace and chapel).

The museum occupies the 17th-century Casa Clariana-Padellàs, a merchant's house that was brought here, stone by stone, in 1930 after the nearby Via Laietana was driven through the Old Town. In the process of re-erecting the house, Roman remains were discovered beneath the ground, and now a huge area of the foundations of the Roman city has been opened up beneath the square. A lift takes visitors down to this sub-terranean city, which shows streets of shops and industries, from textile dyeing to wine-making.

These ancient stones also chart the development of the first Christian palace that stood between the 6th and 8th centuries here, prefiguring the palace of the Barcelona count-kings.

Palau Reial Major

Emerging from this Roman twilight, you arrive at the **Palau Reial Major**, the former royal palace, dominated by the **Saló del Tinell**, the great hall and throne room. Its enormous interior stone arches were designed in the 14th century for Pere III (the Ceremonious) by Guillem Carbonell, who was also responsible for much of the palace's façade. Christopher Columbus is said to have been received in the Tinell by Ferdinand and Isabella. Nowadays, it is used for concerts and exhibitions.

The **Capella Reial de Santa Agata** (Royal Chapel of St Agatha), built for Jaume II (the Just) in 1312, features a rare embellishment in an otherwise rather austere complex. Jaume's coat of arms can be seen behind the retable of the Epiphany, painted by Jaume Huguet in 1464–5, while scenes of St Agatha's martyrdom are depicted in a chapel on the left.

ENDING THE WALK

Return to the front of the Museu d'Història de le Ciutat, where quirky small shops include, at no. 7, the candle-makers **Cereria Subirà**, the oldest shop in the city. Stop for a drink or a chocolate and *xurros* (*churros* – fried snacks made of batter) at the quaint **Mesón del Café**, see ⑪⑥, or just grab a sandwich at **Il Panetto**, see ⑪⑦, around the corner on Carrer de la Tapineria. Alternatively, pick up a pastry from one of *pastelerieas* in this area: *tartaletas de music* ('music' tarts – mixed-nut tartlets) or *empanadas catalanas* (pies filled with tuna and olives) are specialities.

Barcino Wine
Roman Barcino was known for its fish paste *(garum)* and inexpensive wine, Vi de le Laietanis, which travelled well – evidence of it has been found all over Europe. In Roman times, half to three-quarters of a litre (1–1½ pints) of wine was the daily intake.

Food and Drink
⑤ CAFE D'ESTIU
Plaça de Sant Iu 5–6; tel: 93 310 30 14; closed Mon; €
This shaded café in the courtyard outside the Museu Frederic Marès serves decent snacks. The name, meaning 'summer café', in Catalan, reflects the fact that it is open only from May to September.

⑥ MESÓN DEL CAFÉ
Carrer de la Llibreteria 16; tel: 93 315 07 54; €
This quaint little café has been going since 1909. Perch on a bar stool for a delicious coffee or thick, rich hot chocolate and *xurros*.

⑦ IL PANETTO
Carrer de la Tapineria 4; tel: 93 268 30 04; €
In the street that runs beside the Roman wall and the palace, this hole-in-the-wall is a good stop-off point for sandwiches, juices and home-made cakes.

OFFICIAL BARRI GÒTIC

This tour of the Gothic quarter centres on the government buildings on the area's main square, Plaça de Sant Jaume, and also takes in the Jewish quarter. In the surrounding streets you will find some of the city's most engaging old shops.

Above from left:
rose window in
Santa Maria del
Pi; Catalonia and
Spanish flags on top
of the Palau de la
Generalitat, on Plaça
de Sant Jaume, heart
of the administrative
part of the Barri Gòtic.

> **DISTANCE** 2km (1¼ miles)
> **TIME** 3–4 hours
> **START** Pla de la Boqueria
> **END** Carrer de Ferran/La Rambla
> **POINTS TO NOTE**
> It is easy to feel disorientated in the narrow streets of this quarter, but rest assured that you will never be far from Plaça de Sant Jaume on this roughly circular walk.

Halfway down La Rambla by the Liceu metro, the dragon on the Casa Bruno Quadras *(see pp.32–3)* on **Pla de la Boqueria** ❶ marks the corner of Carrer del Cardenal Casañas. This lane of book- and print-sellers sets the tone for the walk and leads into one of the most characterful parts of the Barri Gòtic.

SANTA MARIA DEL PI

Among the highlights of the Barri Gòtic are **Plaça del Pi** and the adjacent **Plaça de Sant Josep Oriol**. Dominating both squares is the large 14th-century Catalan-Gothic **Santa Maria del Pi** ❷. The basilica is distinguished by its stained glass (including a very fine rose window), much of it replaced after being destroyed in 1936 during the Civil War. Joseph Oriol (1650–1702), a local miracle-working priest, is buried here.

Plaça del Pi's handsome domestic architecture includes the pargeting

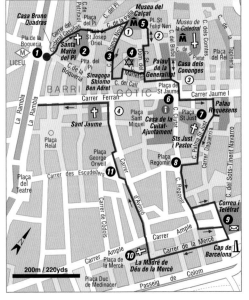

> ## Food and Drink 🍴
> **① EL PORTALON**
> Carrer de Banys Nous, 20; tel:
> 93 302 11 87; €
> This is a typical *bodega* with wine barrels and tapas, though it is not the all-male reserve it once was. Offers good value and authentic ambience.

(raised decorative plasterwork) on the side of the Hotel del Pi and a wonderful stainless-steel Modernista façade on La Gavineteria Roca, purveyors of cut-throat razors since 1911.

Carrers de Petritxol and de la Palla

In the northwest corner of Plaça del Pi is **Carrer de Petritxol**, a little street of art galleries and independent shops. Sala Parés, at no. 5, dates from 1845 and was the first gallery to exhibit work by Pablo Picasso. **Carrer de la Palla**, off Plaça de Sant Josep Oriol, is lined with antiques stores (with the focus on tiles and ceramics) and bookshops, such as Angel Batlle, at no. 23, which also has a wide selection of old prints.

Carrer de Banys Nous

Halfway up Carrer de la Palla take a right turn down **Carrer de Banys Nous ❸**, a delightful street with further antiques stores and bric-à-brac sellers. There is also an atmospheric *bodega*, **El Portalon**, see ⑪①, a cosy *granja (see right)* at no. 20, and, at no. 11, Artesania Catalunya, home to crafts workshops. At the end of the street, on the corner of Carrer del Call, is the hat shop Orbach, selling Borsolinos and genuine Catalan berets.

JEWISH QUARTER

The narrow, sunless lanes between Plaça del Pi and Plaça de Sant Jaume are redolent of medieval Barcelona. Here, the pleasure is simply in walking the streets, peering into patios, window shopping, menu reading and wondering at the history heaped up behind walls of solid stone.

Much of this area was the *call*, or Jewish quarter – the word comes from the Hebrew *qahqal*, meaning 'meeting' – with a large Jewish population here from the 12th century until 1391. That year, following widescale rioting in the wake of accusations that the Jews had brought the plague to Spain, the *call* was virtually destroyed, many of its residents murdered, and the rest given the choice of conversion or expulsion. A century later all non-Catholic religions were banned altogether.

The Synagogue

Turn left into Carrer del Call, then first left and first right into Carrer Marlet. Set within the wall of no. 1 is a Hebrew memorial stone, which dates to 1314 and reads simply, 'Holy foundation of Rabbi Samuel Hassardi for whom life never ends. Year 62'.

Milk Stop
The Barri Gòtic is known for its *granges* (or *granjas*), literally 'dairies'. These traditional cafés sell mainly milk-based drinks, including *orxata*, a thick beverage made with milk and tiger nuts. *Granges* usually also have a good selection of pastries.

Below: one of many antiques shops in the Barri Gòtic.

Big Foot
An attraction in the Museu del Calçat is a huge pair of shoes made to fit the statue of Christopher Columbus *(see p.33),* at the bottom of the Rambla. According to the *Guinness Book of Records,* these are the largest shoes in the world.

At no. 5 is the restored medieval **Sinagoga Shlomo Ben Adret** ❹ (tel: 93 317 07 90; www.calldebarcelona.org; Mon–Fri 11am–6pm, Sat, Sun 11am–3pm; charge), once the largest synagogue in the city.

Museu del Calçat

Carrer Marlet leads into Carrer de Sant Domènec del Call, where you should turn left and stroll up to the attractive, shady **Plaça de Sant Felip Neri** ❺. At no. 5 is what was once the location of the shoemakers' guild, now home to the **Museu del Calçat** (Museum of the History of Footwear; tel: 93 301 45 33; Tue–Sun 11am–2pm; charge), which showcases the history of the craft from Roman times to the present day. Highlights include the largest shoe in the world *(see left)*

If you are in need of a pitstop after you have toured the museum, the **Hotel Neri**, see ⑪②, is a good choice.

Food and Drink 🍴

② **HOTEL NERI**
Carrer de Sant Sever 5; tel: 93 304 06 55; www.hotelneri.com; €€
Try the bar on the top-floor terrace of this 18th-century mansion, now a boutique hotel. Great views over the Gothic quarter.

③ **CAN CONESA**
Plaça de Sant Jaume 10; tel: 93 310 13 94; €
A popular place on the corner of Carrer de la Llibreteria and a good choice for their famously delicious, inexpensive hot sandwiches, with fillings including tortilla or ham and tomato. It's open right from breakfast, and there are often queues in the evenings.

④ **EL GRAN CAFÉ**
Carrer d'Avinyó 9; tel: 93 318 79 86; €€€
This historic café, reminiscent of a classic Parisian Art Nouveau brasserie, has a handsome Modernista interior with huge chandeliers. Rather expensive but has a good-value set lunch.

PLAÇA DE SANT JAUME

Carrer del Call emerges at the **Plaça de Sant Jaume** ❻, the administrative heart of the city, where the Roman Forum once stood. The square is a focal point for celebrations and also has a good place for a snack, see ⑪③.

Palau de la Generalitat

The left-hand side of the square is dominated by the imposing Gothic-and-Renaissance **Palau de la Generalitat** (tel: 93 402 46 17; www.gencat.net; tours every 30 mins; free), from which Catalonia is governed. The building is topped by a statue of St George, the patron saint of Catalonia, and is decked with red roses (and opened to the public) on his saint's day: 23 April. The 15th-century chapel by Marc Safont and the first-floor **Patí dels Tarongers** (Orange Tree Patio, sometimes used for concerts) are among its highlights.

The lane leading up the right-hand side of the Generalitat is the Carrer del Bisbe. On the right is the 14th-century **Casa dels Canonges** (Canons' House), now Generalitat offices. A neo-Gothic bridge, based on the Venetian Bridge of Sighs, links the two buildings.

Ajuntament

Facing the Generalitat on Plaça de Sant Jaume is the **Ajuntament**, or Casa de la Ciutat, Barcelona's town hall (for visits, enquire at the tourist information office on the ground floor). The entrance is flanked by the figures of Jaume I and Joan Fiveller, a 15th-century councillor who established city

freedoms. The building's two most notable rooms are the 14th-century Saló del Consell de Cent, which plays host to concerts, and the Saló de les Cròniques, where, in 1928, Josep Maria Sert painted scenes from the 14th-century Catalan expedition to Byzantium.

SOUTH OF SANT JAUME

Leave Plaça de Sant Jaume down Carrer de Jaume I, taking the second right into Carrer de Dagueria, where you should peek in at Casa Oliveras, on the left, to see lacemakers at work in the shop. This lane leads into **Plaça de Sant Just** ❼, a quiet square overlooked by the large church of **Sants Just i Pastor**.

An alley opposite leads down to **Palau Requesens**, home to the Reial Acadèmia de Bones Lletres, built against the **Roman wall**, which runs down Carrer del Sots-Tinent Navarro.

Head down Carrer de la Palma Sant Just and turn right at the bottom onto **Plaça del Regomir** ❽. On the left, note part of the Roman city's southern gate.

Continue down to Carrer d'en Cignas or Carrer Ample (both good at tapas time), and turn right for the **Correu i Telègraf** ❾ (post office). It is worth popping inside to admire its decoration by *Noucentiste* artists Canyellas, Galí, Labarta and Obiols.

Outside is **Cap de Barcelona** *(see pp.56–7)*, a 64-m (210-ft) cartoon-like portrait of a woman's head by American Pop artist Roy Lichtenstein, finished in 1992. Inspired by Gaudí, the work is made from broken tiles.

La Madre de Déu de la Mercè

Walk back down Carrer de la Mercè to the church of **La Madre de Déu de la Mercè** ❿ (Plaça de la Mercè; tel: 93 315 27 56; daily 10am–1pm, 6–8pm; free), topped by a statue of the Madonna and child that can be seen from out to sea.

La Mercè is the patron saint of Barcelona, and on her saint's day of 24 September, huge models, known as 'giants', and human pyramids (locals, standing on each other's shoulders) greet the dignitaries coming out from Mass at the start of the festivities.

Carrer d'Avinyó

From the church, head back up **Carrer d'Avinyó**, home to two city landmarks: La Manual Alpargatera, at no. 7, which sells espadrilles, and the Modernista **El Gran Café**, see ⑪④. Halfway down on the right is **Plaça George Orwell** ⑪, named after the author of *Homage to Catalonia*.

Turn left at the top of Carrer d'Avinyó, into the shopping street of Carrer de Ferran, which takes you back to La Rambla.

SANT PERE

An enticing marriage of old and new, this eastern corner of the Old Town, north-west of El Born, is where the rag trade once flourished. Its highlights include the Palau de la Música Catalana and the Mercat de Santa Caterina.

DISTANCE 3km (2 miles)
TIME 3 hours
START Palau de la Música
END Mercat de Santa Caterina
POINTS TO NOTE
This walk is best done in the morning, both to avoid the queues at the Palau de la Música Catalana and to arrive at the Mercat de Santa Caterina in time for lunch. Note that the market closes for a few hours in the afternoon from Monday to Wednesday.

In the city's Golden Age of the 14th century, Sant Pere was the residential area of choice among the city's wealthy merchants. As the centre of Barcelona's textile trade, it flourished, but mass-production from the late 19th century led to its demise. Tourists have only recently started exploring its historic streets. This tour reveals its highlights.

PALAU DE LA MÚSICA

Start at the **Palau de la Música Catalana ❶** (Carrer de St Francesc de Paula

Above: details of the exterior of the Palau de la Música Catalana.

Did You Know?
Carrer d'Allada-Vermell is what is described in Barcelona as a 'hard' square, created in 1994 by the demolition of a row of housing to bring light into this dense area.

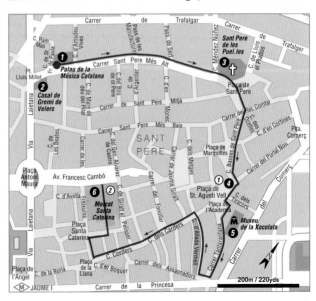

2; tel: 93 295 72 00; www.palaumusica. org; guided tours daily 9.30am–3pm; booking advisable; charge), built in 1908 by architect Domènech i Montaner and now a World Heritage Site. A Modernista extravaganza, it features lavish decoration of tiles, mosaics and statuary reflecting the Catalan musical tradition.

Oscar Tusquets' recent extension, featuring organic motifs in keeping with the Modernista original, houses a concert hall for chamber music and a gourmet restaurant *(see p.121)*. There are tours of the building, which allow you to admire the stained glass and sculptural decoration of the main auditorium.

SANT PERE MÉS ALT

Opposite the Palau, at Carrer Sant Pere Més Alt 1, is the **Casal de Gremi de Velers ❷** (Silk Industry Guild), distinguished by fine *esgrafiat* (decorative relief work). Several other textile retailers are based in this street, which was the focus of the medieval trade.

Sant Pere Més Alt terminates at Plaça de Sant Pere and the church of **Sant Pere de les Puel.les ❸**, a former Benedictine monastery. The Modernista fountain in front is by Pere Falqués.

Take the street opposite for **Plaça de St Augusti Vell ❹**, a pleasant little square, and **Bar Mundial**, see ⑪①.

MUSEU DE LA XOCOLATA

Just beyond, down Carrer d'en Tantarantana, is the large terracotta Barcelona Guild of Pastry-Makers, home to the **Museu de la Xocolata ❺** (Carrer del Comerç 36; tel: 93 268 78 78; www. museuxocolata.com; Mon–Sat 10am–7pm, Sun 10am–3pm; charge). It charts the history of chocolate (brought to Europe by Hernán Cortés and the Conquistadors) through chocolate sculptures and photographs, and also runs courses. The shop, needless to say, is irresistible.

MERCAT DE SANTA CATERINA

Cravings sated, take **Carrer d'Allada Vermell** opposite and turn left at the top into Carrer dels Carders. Continue until you reach Plaça de la Lana, where the Jocs Florals *(see p.22)* were revived in the 20th century, then right for the **Mercat de Santa Caterina ❻** (Mon 7.30am–2pm, Tue–Wed, Sat 7.30am–3.30pm, Thur–Fri 7.30am–8.30pm).

This stunning three-storey building by the late Enric Miralles (architect of the Scottish Parliament), built on the site of a Domenican monastery, is the centre of urban renewal in the area. Its wonderful roof has coloured tiles above and wood below, in arches like upturned boats. Head inside and enjoy a meal at the **Cuines**, see ⑪②.

Above from far left: inside the Modernista Palau de la Música Catalana; Mercat de Santa Caterina.

Above: stained glass in the church of Sant Pere.

Food and Drink

① BAR MUNDIAL

Plaça de St Augusti Vell 1; tel: 93 319 90 56; €
Opened in 1955 and little changed, this neighbourhood classic does great tapas, with particularly tasty seafood.

② CUINES DE SANTA CATERINA

Avinguda de Francesc Cambó 20; tel: 93 268 99 18; €€€
Sit at the bar for a drink and tapas or, for a heartier meal, at one of the tables in this emporium within the market. The week's menu is printed on the paper place settings. Market-fresh food.

LA RIBERA AND EL BORN

The part of the Old Town north of the Via Laietana is La Ribera, a former noble quarter whose name (the shore) reflects its commercially advantageous waterfront position; within La Ribera is El Born. History mixes with fashion and culture here, with chic boutiques, bars and some of the city's top museums.

Above: the excellent Museu Picasso.

DISTANCE 3km (2 miles)
TIME 4 hours
START Jaume I metro
END Estació de França
POINTS TO NOTE
Start early to avoid the queues at the Museu Picasso (free on the first Sunday of the month). This walk combines well with the tour of the adjacent Sant Pere *(see p.44)*.

This close-knit residential area owes its character to Jaume I (the Conqueror), under whom Catalonia flourished in its Golden Age of the 14th century. The city's rich were businessmen, not aristocrats, and it was in this waterfront area that merchants brought their wares ashore. They traded in the new stock exchange, prayed in Santa Maria del Mar (the church they swiftly had built in gratitude), jousted on the tilting

Street Names
Many streets in this area are named after *gremis*, the powerful trade guilds, whose duty was to look after the interests of their members. These include Agullers (needle makers), Argenteria (silver-smiths) and Som-breres (hatmakers).

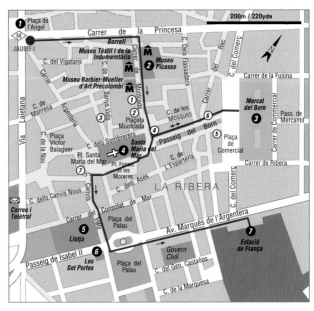

field of El Born and entertained in the sumptuous mansions they erected, notably along Carrer de Montcada.

In later times, a young Pablo Picasso studied at the local art school, where his father also taught; nowadays the Museu Picasso is the area's big crowd-puller.

CARRER MONTCADA

Start at the **Jaume I metro ❶** and stroll down Carrer de la Princesa, which divides the Sant Pere district *(see p.44)* from La Ribera. At **Borrell**, an old-fashioned chocolate shop, turn right into the slim **Carrer de Montcada**. Named after the fallen in the conquest of Mallorca, it linked the waterfront with the commercial areas during the city's Golden Age, and the architecturally lavish Catalan Gothic merchants' mansions that line it reflect its former wealth. Montcada has become museum street supreme, since the authorities started renovating its medieval palaces in 1957.

There are lots of good pitstops near here, such as **Espai Barroc**, see ⑪①, or **El Xampanyet**, see ⑪②.

Museu Picasso

At Carrer de Montcada 15–23 is the **Museu Picasso ❷** (tel: 93 319 63 10; www.museupicasso.bcn.es; Tue–Sun 10am–8pm; last admission 30 mins before closing; charge), spread over five imposing mansions. The entrance is at no. 15, the Palau Berenguer d'Aguilar, with a handsome courtyard and first-floor gallery by Marc Safont, architect of the inner patio of the Generalitat. This mansion is connected internally to Palau del Baró de Balaguer at no. 17, Palau Meca at no. 19, and then Casa Mauri and Palau Finestres, the last two used for temporary exhibitions.

There are some 3,000 artworks in the collection, mainly from Picasso's formative years, with sketches in school books and a masterly portrait of his mother, done when he was just 16. Studies for *Las Meninas* from the 1950s are among the few later works. The museum also has an attractive café.

Museu Tèxtil

Opposite the Museu Picasso, at no. 12, is the **Museu Tèxtil i de la Indumentària** (tel: 93 319 76 03; www.museu textil.bcn.es; Tue–Sat 10am–6pm, Sun 10am–3pm; charge). Housed in the two adjoining palaces, it has a small collection of textiles and fashions from the 14th century to the present, including items by Balenciaga, Pucci and Chanel. There is a gift shop, and the courtyard makes a lovely setting for the museum's **Café Tèxtil**, which stays open till late.

Above from far left:
Museu Picasso sign; admiring the collection; Santa Maria del Mar; colourful sign for the Museu Tèxtil.

Above: exhibits at the Museu Tèxtil.

Food and Drink 🍴

① ESPAI BARROC
Carrer de Montcada 20; tel: 93 310 06 73; €€
A cultural highlight in the Palau Dalmases is this Baroque-style bar. The piped music is opera, and there are live recitals on Thursdays.

② EL XAMPANYET
Carrer de Montcada 22; tel: 93 319 70 03; €€
Wash down the house speciality, anchovies, with cava, served in wide-brimmed glasses. Tiny bar with a big atmosphere.

Montcada Fresco
A fresco of Jaume I's campaign on the island of Mallorca has been taken from the wall of one of the mansions in Carrer de Montcada and can now be seen in the Palau Nacional *(see p.75)*.

Late Starters
The atmosphere
in this area is
transformed at night:
bars that during
the day are hidden
behind closed doors
or lurk in stygian
gloom start to wake
up at around 9pm,
and the merry-go-
round of tireless bar-
flies continues until
about 4am.

Below: colourful El
Born backstreet.

Other Montcada Galleries

At Carrer de Montcada 14, next door
to the Museu Tèxtil, is the **Museu Bar-
bier-Mueller d'Art Precolombí** (tel:
93 310 45 16; www.barbier-mueller.ch;
Tue–Sat 10am–6pm, Sun 10am–3pm;
charge). What the collection of Pre-
Columbian art lacks in size, it more
than compensates for in terms of pres-
tige, with superb Aztec, Mayan and
Inca jewellery and artefacts.

Continue along the street for two
contemporary art galleries that usually have notable exhibitions: **Sala
Montcada**, also at no. 14, is run by
the culturally aware La Caixa savings
bank, who mount shows of Spanish
and international artists here; and
Galeria Maeght, housed in the Palau
Cervelló at no. 25, is part of the French
Maeght gallery group, which owes its
success to its early support in Cannes
of Provence-based artists Matisse,
Bonnard, Van Dongen and Miró.

EL BORN

Carrer de Montcada ends at Plaçeta de
Montcada, where it hits the **Passeig
del Born**. Nearby, on Carrer de Banys
Vells, parallel to Montcada, is the
excellent historic wine bar **Va de Vi**,
see ⑪③. The main strip here is a fash-
ionistas' haunt, home to chic bars and
cafés (see ⑪④, ⑪⑤ and ⑪⑥), popular night spots *(see left)* and numerous
designer boutiques.

Mercat del Born

A detour east along Passeig del Born
takes you past Carrer dels Flassaders
(on your left), where there are more
boutiques, and, at the end of the Passeig, Josep Fontserè i Mestre's 19th-
century wrought-iron **Mercat del
Born ❸**, until 1971, a wholesale food
market. The structure is being remodelled as a cultural centre, but work has
been delayed due to the discovery
during renovation of pre-18th-century
houses on the site. A viewing platform
can be accessed on Carrer de la Fusina,
on the market's northern edge.

SANTA MARIA DEL MAR

At the western end of Passeig del Born
is **Santa Maria del Mar ❹** (tel: 93 310
23 90; Mon–Sat 9.30am–1.30pm,
4.30–8pm, Sun 4.30–8pm; free), built
from 1329 to 1384 by the maritime
enterprises that brought wealth to this
part of town. It is a fine example of the
Catalan-Gothic style of architecture,
with its horizontal lines, flat terraced
roofing, wide open spaces and octagonal

towers. Stand by the main door to appreciate the sense of space and the warm light that enters through the 15th-century rose window. The striking blue window in the second chapel on the left in the ambulatory commemorates the 1992 Olympic Games.

Surrounding Squares

In **Plaça Fossar de les Moreres**, the square beside the church, note the iron monument topped by a flame; this commemorates the martyrs of the Bourbon succession in 1714. Beyond it, **Plaça de Santa Maria del Mar** is a buzzy square with appealing cafés and bars, such as **La Vinya del Senyor**, see ⑪⑦. Just to the right is **Carrer de l'Argenteria**, one of the busiest restaurant streets in town, where there are regular queues in the evening, as people wait to get into the popular tapas bars and restaurants here.

THE LLOTJA

On the opposite (port) side of the square, turn down Carrer dels Canvis Vells, which leads to the Carrer del Consolat de Mar and the **Llotja** ❺ (closed to visitors), the former stock exchange – a handsome 14th-century building with a magnificent Gothic hall.

Picasso's father taught at the Escola de Belles Arts (School of Fine Arts) that occupied the upper part of the building. The **Reial Academia Catalana de Belles Arts de Sant Jordi** (visits on request: museu@racba.org) still occupies part of the building. Its small museum has drawings by the 19th-century Romantic painter Mariano Fortuny.

Les Set Portes

Across the busy Passeig de Isabel II, in an arcaded 19th-century building, is Barcelona's most famous restaurant, **Les Set Portes** ❻ *(see p.121)*. Peek through the windows to see the handsome panelled interior and imagine Picasso, Lorca and the rest of the artistic crowd enjoying a dish of its speciality black rice or paella.

Further along the road is the grand **Estació de França** ❼ *(see right)*, the city's original international train terminus, now restored, and well worth a look in for its handsome iron-and-glass 19th-century structure.

Church Concerts

Concerts, from classical to jazz, are held in the church of Santa Maria del Mar *(above)*. Check the church notice board for details.

Food and Drink 🍴

③ VA DE VI
Carrer de Banys Vells 16; tel: 93 319 29 00; €
Cavernous old wine bar with a modern designer touch. Great place to try the best of Spain's wines and local artisanal produce.

④ EUSKAL ETXEA
Plaçeta de Montcada 1–3; tel: 93 310 21 85; €€€
Superb Basque tapas bar and cultural centre. Full meals also available in the restaurant.

⑤ PITIN BAR
Passeig del Born 34; tel: 93 319 50 87; €
Well-established little bar, where the house speciality is *pitin,* tea with steamed milk.

⑥ LA TAVERNA DEL BORN
Passeig del Born, 27; tel: 93 315 09 64; €€
Great at any time of day for drinks, snacks and people-watching.

⑦ LA VINYA DEL SENYOR
Plaça de Santa Maria 5; tel: 93 310 33 79; €€€
The Lord's Vineyard is a classic wine bar in a great spot on the square. Excellent tapas and an incredibly wide selection of wines.

EL RAVAL

The city's old working-class district still has a slightly raw edge that is reminiscent of a seedy past, but urban redevelopment has laid out new spaces and a fabulous contemporary art museum, the MACBA.

DISTANCE 2.5km (1½ miles)
TIME 2 hours
START La Rambla (top end)
END Palau Güell
POINTS TO NOTE
This walk runs parallel to La Rambla, on its southwestern side. It is best to do it during the daytime, but not on Tuesday, when MACBA (the Contemporary Art Museum) is closed.

Lively Nightlife
El Raval comes to life at night, with a variety of bars and clubs, such as Rita Blue in Plaça de Sant Augustí or Aurora on the Rambla del Raval, where arthouse short films form a hip backdrop.

On the opposite side of La Rambla to the Barri Gòtic is the working-class area of the city that was incorporated into the Old Town with the building of the medieval city walls.

El Raval (literally, 'the slum') stretches across from La Rambla to the Ronda de Sant Pau and the Avinguda del Paral.lel. The district of old high-rise tenements was once one of the world's most densely populated areas, with many immigrants from the poorer regions of Spain housed here.

The area towards the waterfront was a haunt of sailors, delinquents and addicts. In the 1920s it was dubbed the *Barri Xinès* (*Barrio Chino* in Spanish), meaning Chinese quarter, though the Chinese were never in evidence here.

Food and Drink 🍴
① CAMPER FOOD BALL
Carrer d'Elisabets 9; tel: 93 270 13 63; €
The popular Barcelona shoe firm have branched out into 'food balls', basically a main course or dessert of all-natural ingredients in a ball.

② BIOCENTER
Carrer del Pintor Fortuny 25; tel: 93 301 45 83; €
This well-established, friendly vegetarian restaurant does healthy, hearty four-course set-price menus.

Regeneration Area

The area is undergoing a metamorphosis, thanks to municipal funding. Trendy bars, shops and art galleries now sit side by side with more seedy spots: do not be surprised at the sight of sex workers on street corners in the broad light of day. Regeneration has been in progress in El Raval since the late 1990s, with whole blocks of tenements coming down to open up the area. There is still a large immigrant population here (over 50 per cent are from outside Spain), making it one of the most ethnically diverse parts of Europe.

MACBA

From the top of La Rambla, take the second right down Carrer del Bonsucces and Carrer d'Elisabets. Like all the streets in this area, it retains many good traditional bars and some quirky new restaurants; recommendations include the new-style **Camper Food Ball**, see ①① and, on the parallel street Carrer Pintor Fortuny, the **Biocenter**, see ①②.

Follow the signs to Plaça dels Àngels and architect Richard Meier's ice-white Modernist-style **Museu d'Art Contemporani de Barcelona ❶** (MACBA; tel: 93 412 08 10; www.macba.es; Oct–May: Mon, Wed–Fri 11am–7.30pm, Sat 10am–8pm, Sun 10am–3pm, June–Sept: Mon, Wed–Sat 11am–8pm, Sun 10am–3pm; charge), at no. 1, with the neighbouring Convent dels Àngels acting as an outpost. The front slopes are popular with skate-boarders.

On Thursdays in summer (July–Sept) MACBA remains open until midnight, allowing art lovers in at the reduced price of €3. Concerts are also often held in the bar on these late nights.

The Collection

Arranged over three floors, the gallery (opened in 1995) showcases post-war Catalan, Spanish and international art from c.1950, with works by artists including Antonio Saura, Tàpies, Joseph Beuys, Jeff Wall and Susana Solano. The permanent collection is displayed on a rotating basis, but the main attraction is generally the cutting-edge temporary exhibitions by comtemporary artists. La Central del MACBA is the museum's bookshop-cum-reference centre. **Capella MACBA** is the convent's 15th-century Gothic church with the only Renaissance chapel in Barcelona.

CENTRE DE CULTURA CONTEMPORÀNIA

This melding of ancient and modern, at which the Barcelonans are so good, can be seen again at the Plaça de Joan Coromines, which links the MACBA with the old Casa de Caritat, formerly a poorhouse and orphanage that has become the magnificent, four-storey **Centre de Cultura Contemporània de Barcelona ❷** (CCCB; Carrer de Montalegre 5; tel: 93 306 41 00; www.cccb.org; mid-Sept–mid-June: Tue, Thur, Fri 11am–2pm, 4–8pm, Wed, Sat 11am–8pm, Sun 11am–7pm; mid-June–mid-Sept: Tue–Sat 11am–8pm,

Above from far left: façade *(left)*, visitors *(centre left)*, artworks *(centre right)* and skate-boarders *(right)* at the Museu de Art Contemporani de Barcelona.

Theatre Street
Avinguda del Paral.lel, on the south side of El Raval, was once renowned as Europe's 'Street of Theatres'. Famous for vaudeville, music halls and cabaret, its most famous venue was El Molino (The Windmill), called the Petit Moulin Rouge after its Parisian counterpart, though it changed its name when 'red' became an unwise word to use during the Franco era. Opened in 1899, it did not quite manage to see out the 20th century. Other, larger theatres remain, most showing musicals or farces that attract coach parties from out of town.
The street name, Paral.lel, supplanted the existing Calle Marques de Duero in 1794, when a Frenchman, Pierre François André Méchain, discovered that the avenue lay exactly along the parallel latitude 44° 44' North.

Sun 11am–3pm; charge). The centre, which is entered via a ramp in the basement, puts on exhibitions, concerts, dance and films.

Also on Plaça de Joan Coromines is a new university faculty building and the **Centre d'Estudis i Recursos Culturals** (CERC; tel: 93 402 25 65; www.diba.es/cerc; free). Step inside to see the lovely, tiled 18th-century courtyard, **Pati Manning**, with an Art Deco St George, and perhaps have an inexpensive tapas or drink in the courtyard's café.

At the back of the courtyard is a last vestige of religiosity in the area, the church of **Santa Maria de Montealegre**, where Mass is still held.

ANTIC HOSPITAL DE LA SANTA CREU

At this point walk back down Carrer dels Àngels to the 15th-century **Antic Hospital de la Santa Creu ❸** (Carrer del Carme 47–Carrer de l'Hospital 56;

no tel; Mon–Fri 9am–8pm, Sat 9am–2pm; free), a convalescent house set up in the 15th century and the city's principal hospital until 1910, when Santa Creu i Sant Paul was built near the Sagrada Família *(see p.70).*

Some of the building is used to house archives and as the headquarters of the Royal Academy of Medicine, but the complex is otherwise devoted to the Massana Art School, the Institute of Catalan Studies and the Library of Catalonia.

On the right as you enter is the Casa de Convalescència (Convalescence House), its gardens richly decorated with 17th-century Baroque tiles by Llorens Passolles. This first square is named after Alexander Fleming, who discovered penicillin, and a statue of the great man stands just outside.

Exit through the main entrance in Carrer de l'Hospital. Just outside is **La Capella** (Tue–Sat noon–2pm, 4–8pm; free), the hospital's 15th-century chapel, now an exhibition space for contemporary art.

Carrer de l'Hospital

On **Carrer de l'Hospital** are characterful small shops such as herbalists, pharmacists and Arab pastry stores, reflecting the quirky mix of traditional and ethnic in this area. One of its side streets, the pedestrian Carrer de la Riera Baixa, is lined with second-hand clothes shops. At the northern end of this street is Carrer de la Riera Alta, worth a detour if you need a pitstop, for **El Café que Pone Muebles Navarra**, see ❸.

Above: Sant Pau del Camp.

Slaughtered

Barcelona's industrial legacy is nearly gone. West of El Raval, the former city slaughter house, the Excorxador, is marked by Joan Miró's coloured tile totem, *Dona i Ocell* (Woman and Bird, *illustrated on p.26, bottom left*).

Food and Drink 🍴

③ EL CAFE QUE PONE MUEBLES NAVARRA
Carrer de la Riera Alta 4–6; tel: 93 442 39 66; €
Large, quirky bar with comfy seating in a former furniture store. Ideal as a place to put your feet up for a coffee or cocktail.

④ LONDON BAR
Nou de la Rambla 34; tel: 027 771 63 23; €
Apart from the addition of a big television screen, this historic pub (est. 1910) has changed little since Miró and Picasso drank here.

⑤ BAR PASTIS
Carrer de Santa Monica 4; tel: 93 318 79 80; €
This atmospheric little bar is crammed with Edith Piaf memorabilia. The music theme continues with regular live performances: French song (Sun), Tango (Tue) and singer/songwriters (Wed).

Back on Carrer de l'Hospital, head west on to Carrer de Sant Antoni Abat, which extends to **Mercat de Sant Antoni ❹**, a large, attractive 19th-century market hall. During the week this serves as a food market, with clothes and haberdashers' stalls behind the encircling green blinds, and on Sunday, from 8am–2pm, it is given over to a lively market for second-hand books, coins and videos.

Rambla del Raval

Walking back along Carrer de Sant Antoni Abat and into Carrer de l'Hospital will bring you to the top of the **Rambla del Raval ❺**. This tree-lined thoroughfare was only recently created by bulldozing more than five blocks through the heart of the *Barri Xinès*, but it is already bringing wealth to the area in the shape of bars, galleries and cafés attracting a bohemian crowd.

SANT PAU DEL CAMP

At the bottom of the Rambla del Raval, turn right into Carrer de Sant Pau to reach **Sant Pau del Camp ❻** (tel: 93 441 00 01; Mon–Fri noon–1pm, 7.30–8.30pm; charge), at no. 101. This is Barcelona's oldest church, dating back to Roman times. The name, meaning 'of the field', refers to when the area was in the countryside.

A door to the right leads to a small, pretty cloister with trefoil and cinquefoil arches. A gravestone, used first for a Roman, bears an inscription to Guifre II Borrell, who in 897 became the second ruler of the Barcelona dynasty.

PALAU GÜELL

Finally, walk down Carrer Nou de la Rambla, past the **London Bar**, see ⑪④, to the **Palau Güell ❼** (Carrer Nou de la Rambla 3; tel: 93 317 39 74; closed for renovation until 2009), designed by Gaudí from 1885–9 as a town house for his patron, Count Eusebi Güell.

With this building, the architect embarked on a period of fertile creativity, alternating elements of the Gothic with Arabic design. The house is structured around an enormous salon, from which a conical roof covered in pieces of tiling emerges to preside over an unusual landscape of capriciously placed battlements, balustrades and strangely shaped chimneys.

Two streets down from Palau Güell is **Bar Pastis**, see ⑪⑤, a good choice for a drink to round off the tour.

Above from far left: El Raval bookshop; trendy bar.

Did You Know?
Although Eusebi Güell lived in his Palau Güell for two years, he apparently never visited the extraordinary roof, decorated with multi-coloured chimneys in Gaudí's characteristic broken-tile mosaic, known as *trencadis*.

Below: local barbers.

THE WATERFRONT

Rejuvenated for the Barcelona Olympic Games in 1992, the waterfront area has added an exciting new dimension to the city. This tour takes you through Port Vell (Old Port) and the regenerated area of Barceloneta.

DISTANCE 4km (2¼ miles)
TIME 3 hours
START Museu Maritim
END Torre de Jaume I
POINTS TO NOTE

This is a gentle-paced walk that can be done at any time of day or in the evening, although note that the Museu d'Història de Catalunya closes on Monday.

Shipping Links
Barcelona has direct links by ship with the ports in Genoa, Rome, Algiers-Oran, Ibiza, Majorca and Menorca.

Commercial maritime activity moved out of Barcelona's original port in the 1990s, leaving Port Vell, the Old Port, with few concerns other than round-the-clock leisure. A focus of the city, this is where people come to spend idle hours, watching vessels from the yacht clubs pass beneath the swing bridge on the pedestrian Rambla de Mar, seeing who is sipping champagne on the huge posh yachts in the marina, or admiring the visiting tall ships.

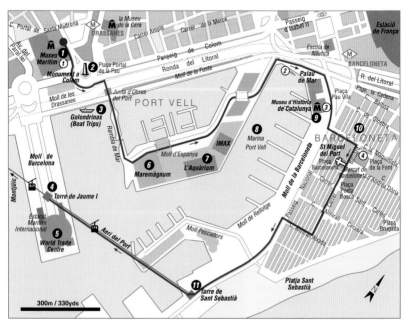

On the north-east (or far) side of the port is Barceloneta, the old fishermen's quarter *(see p.57)*, while on the south side is the cruise-line terminal.

OLD SHIPYARDS

Beyond the bottom of La Rambla are the Drassanes, the city's formidable former shipyards, now home to the Museu Marítim, a good place to begin a tour of waterfront Barcelona.

Proud History

Erected in 1378, enclosed by the city's 15th-century outer wall (which stretches round into Avinguda del Paral.lel, where the Portal de Santa Madrona tower and gateway remain) and greatly enlarged in the 17th century, the huge, shed-like Drassanes launched thousands of ships. At their height they were turning out 30 war galleys at a time, as when the Christian West prepared for a final showdown with the Muslim Ottomans in 1571 at Lepanto off the Greek coast.

Museu Marítim

The **Museu Marítim ❶** (Avinguda de les Drassanes; tel: 93 342 99 20; www.museumaritimbarcelona.com; daily 10am–8pm; charge) charts Catalonia's seafaring history with a fine collection of fishing boats and model ships, a model-making workshop, and reconstructions of wharves, rope-makers' lofts, cabins, agents' offices and artefacts. A full-scale replica of Don Juan of Austria's victorious flagship, the *Reial* (the original of which was built

here), is the centrepiece of the museum. This great gold-trimmed galley, with banks of oars to drive it head-on into its foe, bore the Lepanto Christ, a crucifix now in Barcelona cathedral *(see p.36)*. There is also a café with a garden, shop and restaurant, see ⑪①.

Plaça Portal de la Pau

The nearby Monument a Colom *(see p.29)*, stands in the **Plaça Portal de la Pau ❷** (Gate of Peace Square). It was through a gate on this site that Christopher Columbus most triumphantly entered the city on his return from the West Indies in April 1493.

PORT VELL

Moll de les Drassanes

In front of the statue is the waterfront **Moll de les Drassanes** (*moll* means wharf), from where **Las Golondrinas ❸** ('swallows') pleasure boats (tel: 93 442 31 06; www.lasgolondrinas.com; summer: daily 11.45am–7.30pm; rest of year: slightly shorter hours; charge) run trips to the entrance of the commercial harbour or to the Olympic port.

Food and Drink ⑪

① **CAFETERIA RESTAURANT**
Museu Maritim; Drassanes Reials de Barcelona; tel: 93 31 52 56; open museum hours, plus Thur, Fri and Sat evenings; €€€
The maritime museum's restaurant/café does a wide range of dishes, and has a pleasant outdoor area in the Jardín del Rey. You do not have to visit the museum to get in, but this will get you a 10 per cent discount.

Above from far left: café tables by the port; in the Museu Marítim; cycling along the waterfront; sunbathing on the boardwalk.

Below: the Monument a Colom; yacht in the harbour; one of the Golondrinas.

Did You Know? The Golondrinas have been plying these waters since the 1888 Universal Exhibition. Be sure to choose one of the older and more elegant boats, which have names such as *Mercedes*, *Lolita* and *Encarnación*.

Above: Rambla de Mar footbridge; ship's rigging.

To the left is the **Junta d'Obres del Port**, the Port Authority building constructed in 1907 as a reception point for passengers.

Moll de Barcelona

Today, cruise-line passengers embark at the Moll Adossat further south, but high-speed boats to the Balearics disembark at the Estacio Maritim Internacional on the 500-m (1,640-ft) **Moll de Barcelona**, which runs at right angles to the Moll de Drassanes.

The jetty also has the 119-m (390-ft) **Torre de Jaume I ❹** link for the cross-harbour cable car, the **Aeri del Port**, erected in 1931 and leading from Montjüic; it continues to the Torre de Sant Sebastià *(see opposite)*, at the south-eastern end of the port.

At the end of the Moll de Barcelona is also the **World Trade Centre ❺**, designed by architect I.M. Pei (of Paris's Louvre pyramid fame) and housing a commercial centre with offices, restaurants and a five-star hotel.

Moll d'Espanya

Walk over the undulating wooden Rambla de Mar footbridge to the **Moll d'Espanya**, Port Vell's main jetty. This is a popular place for families and young Barcelonans at weekends and evenings, with the **Maremàgnum ❻** shopping mall, Imax cinema and an aquarium, **L'Aquàrium ❼** (tel: 93 221 74 74; www.aquariumbcn.com; Oct–May: Mon–Fri 9.30am–9pm, Sat, Sun 9.30am–9.30pm, June, Sept: daily 9.30am–9pm, July, Aug: daily 9.30am–11pm; charge). In the aquarium, the blue-shimmering tanks show what swims in the surrounding seas, and a glass tunnel leads visitors among sharks and rays.

Outside the Imax cinema is a replica of Narcís Monturiol's wooden submarine, *Ictineu II,* that entered the waters here in 1864 *(see box right).*

Moll de la Fusta and the Marina

The **Moll d'Espanya** leads ashore to the old timber wharf, the **Moll de la Fusta** (Wood Wharf), redesigned as a palm-lined promenade in the late 1980s by Manuel de Solà-Morales. Next to it, the **Marina Port Vell ❽** is

always bustling with yachts on the move, and here you can climb aboard the **Luz de Gas Port Vell** floating bar, see ⓣ②. Adjacent, in the Porta del Pau is American Pop artist Roy Lichtenstein's colourful *Cap de Barcelona* (Barcelona Head; *see p.43*).

Museu d'Història de Catalunya

In former times this was a dock area that bustled with industry, but the only warehouse remaining is Elies Rogent's 1878 brick-built Magatzem General, now the Palau de Mar. Part of the building is used to house the excellent **Museu d'Història de Catalunya** ❾ (Plaça de Pau Vila 3; tel: 93 221 17 46; www.mhcat.net; Tue, Thur–Sat 10am–7pm; Wed 10am–8pm; Sun 10am–2.30pm; charge). It covers two substantial floors, the first of which takes the story up to the 18th century; the second begins with industrialisation and includes intriguing memories of the Franco years. The museum's rooftop café has a great view over the harbour, see ⓣ③.

BARCELONETA

At the end of the Marina quay is **Barceloneta** ❿, once home to the city's fishing community. The area was created in 1753 to house citizens who had been usurped by the building of the Ciutadella fortress *(see p.59)*, and the architect, military engineer Juan Martin de Cermeño, created two-storey terraces built on a grid system to allow volleys from the castle to be directed down the streets.

Though this is still a close-knit community, its small bars and restaurants have become popular night spots with people from across the city. Its vicinity to the beach also makes it popular, and increasingly flats are being restored to be let out to tourists.

In the heart of the district is a market, designed by Josep Mias and incorporating material from the area's 19th-century market. The market bar, **El Paco**, see ⓣ④, is a good place to stop for snacks. Note also the Moll del Rellotge (Clock Wharf), named after the clock tower (closed to the public) here that once served as a lighthouse.

Cable-Car Ride

An option at this point is to continue walking for around another 15 minutes to the end of the harbour and the **Torre de Sant Sebastià** ⓫. A lift ascends the iron hulk to a platform from which the cable cars fly over the harbour back to the Torre de Jaume I *(see left)*.

Above from far left: the boardwalk by Maremàgnum; Cap de Barcelona; night-time illuminations; cable car over the port.

Helicopter Ride Cat Helicòpters (tel: 93 224 07 10; www.cathelicopters. com) offers 10-minute flights over the city, covering the Olympic sights, Barça football stadium, Tibidabo, Park Güell and the Sagrada Família, the Forum and port. The heliport is located at Moll Adossat, the cruise-ship quay.

An Idealist Inventor

Taking pride of place in the old port is a replica of *Ictineu II*, the world's first combustion-powered submarine. Its inventor was Narcís Monturiol (1819–85), who came up with the design after witnessing the dangerous work of coral divers in Cadaqués. An idealist with socialist beliefs, Monturiol was briefly exiled to France where he met the Icarians, like-minded intellectuals who went on to try to establish Icaria, a Utopian colony in America. It failed, but the name was perpetuated in Barcelona's industrial district, Nova Icària; this became the site of the Olympic Village, where it was hoped that Utopian values might prevail.

CIUTADELLA

Parc de la Ciutadella is the city's favourite open space, a leisurely playground of gardens, boating lake, museums and zoo, making a pleasant escape from the city clamour. To the north you will find the inspiring Museu de la Música and Els Encants, the bustling flea market.

Above: the Catalan parliament building, located within the park; flamingos at the zoo; traffic lights by the Torre Agbar, where the route ends.

DISTANCE 5km (3 miles)
TIME 4 hours
START Arc de Triomf
END Plaça de les Glòries Catalanes

POINTS TO NOTE

This route starts at the Arc de Triomf metro but could begin anywhere in the park. Its second leg could be taken by tram, or as a separate trip.

Next to the Old Town's La Ribera quarter, inland from Barceloneta, lies Parc de la Ciutadella, a large and felicitous green space. An unhurried stroll through the park may be enough of an outing for a visitor, but if you feel energetic it could also be combined with a trip to the Teatre Nacional de Catalunya and the excellent Museu de la Música, as well as to the sprawling flea market of Els Encants at Plaça de les Glòries Catalanes.

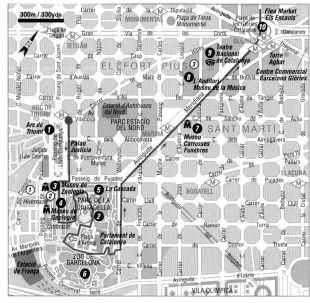

ARC DE TRIOMF

On the north side of the park is the **Arc de Triomf ❶**, by the metro station of the same name. This bulky brick monument, echoing its namesake on the Champs–Élysées in Paris, was designed by Josep Vilaseca i Casanovas as the entrance to the Universal Exhibition of 1888, which was staged in the park. A frieze around the top is peopled with symbolic figures by some of the finest sculptors of the period, including Josep Llimona.

Walk down the Passeig de Lluís Companys, ever-popular with men playing *petanca* (boules). The law courts are on the left, and, if you look back up the avenue, the Collserolla hills provide a grand backdrop. If you want to eat before continuing into the park proper, turn into Carrer del Comerç, on your right, for **Santa Maria**, see ⑪①.

PARC DE LA CIUTADELLA

At the bottom of Passeig de Lluís Companys is the main entrance to the 30-ha (75-acre) **Parc de la Ciutadella ❷** (daily 10am–sunset; free). It is easy to while away time here, in the shade of different deciduous, coniferous and palm trees, all well labelled, and now inhabited by squawking parakeets escaped from cages on La Rambla.

Origins

The park takes its name from a star-shaped citadel built by Felipe V to control the city after his successful siege in 1714 *(see p.24)*. The fortress was later torn down and the park given to the city to turn into a public space by General Prim, when he became Spain's president in 1869, although he was assassinated only a year later. It was laid out by Josep Fontserré (for whom a young Antoni Gaudí worked briefly) in 1873.

Castell dels Tres Dragons

Most of the buildings designed for the 1888 Universal Exhibition were hastily erected and not intended to last. An exception is Modernista architect Lluís Domènech i Montaner's Café-Restaurant, to the right of the park as you enter, and more often known as the **Castell dels Tres Dragons** (Castle of the Three Dragons).

Today a visitor may be forgiven for thinking that this crenellated red-brick fort, modelled on the Llotja (Stock Exchange) in Valencia and impossible to miss, gave the park its name. It never opened as a restaurant but instead served as an arts-and-crafts centre and the architect's studio for a period after the exhibition closed.

A parliament assembled here in 1917, and in 1934 it opened its doors to the **Museu de Zoologia ❸** (tel: 93 319 69 12; www.bcn.es/museusciencies;

Above from far left: the park's monumental Cascada fountain; playground fun; sea lions at the zoo; interior of the Umbracle palm house.

Liberal General
General Prim, who wanted a model monarchy in Spain, once stated, 'Looking for a democratic monarch in Europe is like trying to find an atheist in heaven.'

Food and Drink 🍴

① SANTA MARIA
Carrer del Comerç 17; tel: 93 315 12 27; €€
Young, creative chef Paco Guzman promotes the rare idea of gourmet food at manageable prices, with his dainty but delectable little plates of Mediterranean and Oriental extraction.

Above: exterior of the Umbracle; fountain statue.

Passeig de Picasso
This avenue, which runs along the western edge of the park, was designed by Josep Fontserré as part of the Ciutadella redevelopment. Look out, on the part of the road near the Umbracle, for Antoni Tàpies' 1981 sculpture *Homenatje a Picasso* (Homage to Picasso), enclosed within a glass box. Some good bars and bicycle-hire shops can be found here.

Tue, Wed, Fri–Sun 10am–2pm, Thur 10am–6pm; charge), the home of a collection of stuffed animals as well as host to changing exhibitions.

Museu de Geologia

Further on, on the same side, is the Neoclassical **Museu de Geologia** ❹ (tel: 93 319 69 12; www.bcn.es/museu ciencies; Tue, Wed, Fri–Sun 10am–2pm, Thur 10am–6pm; charge), known together with the zoology museum as the Museu de Ciències Naturals de la Ciutadella. The geology museum houses crystals, minerals and fossils and gives an idea of the landscape around Catalunya, from the volcanic Garrotxa region to the wetlands of the Ebre delta.

Greenhouses, Cascada and Lake

On either side of the Museu de Geologia lie the greenhouses of the **Hivernacle**, an idyllic setting for a café, see Ⓨ②, and summer jazz concerts, and the **Umbracle** palm house.

From here, cross back over the main path to **La Cascada** ❺, a monumental fountain with Neptune, nymphs and grottos by Fontserré. Take a break in front of the fountain at the Cascada Qiosc, where you can buy drinks and snacks. A few steps further on is a boating lake (€2 for 30 mins), where life slows to a ripple, and ducks preen and bask on the banks for your admiration.

Plaça d'Armes

Beyond the lake is the **Plaça d'Armes**, where *El Desconsol* (The Inconsolable), a Josep Llimona damsel, crouches in the central pond. The buildings each side of

the square are all that remain of the citadel built by the victorious Bourbon king, Felipe V. Later used as a prison, the buildings were captured by Napoleon, demolished, rebuilt, handed back to the town, then bombed in the Civil War. On the west side is a chapel and, beside it, the former local governor's palace (1748), which is now a school.

On the opposite, eastern, side of the square is the former **arsenal**, which was made into a royal palace, when the park became a leisure ground in the late 19th century. This is where the **Parlament de Catalunya** sits today, guarded by the Mossos d'Esquadra, the Catalan police.

Parc Zoològic

The main avenue in the park ends at **Plaça del General Prim**, dominated by an equestrian statue of the general. This is also the entrance to the **Zoo de Barcelona** ❻ (tel: 93 225 67 80; www.zoobarcelona.com; daily Apr–Sept: 10am–7pm, Mar, Oct: 10am–6pm, Nov–Feb: 10am–5pm; charge). Its Aquarama dolphin show (hourly at weekends) is the big attraction, although there are also sea lions, elephants, hippos, monkeys and farmyard animals.

NORTH OF THE PARK

There is an exit from the zoo on to **Carrer de Wellington**, where you can catch a tram up Avinguda Meridiana, past the **Museu Carrosses Funebres** ❼ (Carrer de Sancho de Avila 2; tel: 93 484 17 10; Mon–Fri 10am–1pm, 4–6pm, Sat, Sun 10am–1pm; free), near the Marina metro station. One of the city's

more curious museums, it is dedicated to hearses from the 18th century to the 1950s, and claims to have more than anywhere else in the world.

L'Auditori

Alight at the same metro stop for Rafael Moneo's 1999 **L'Auditori** ❽ (Carrer de Lepant 150; tel: 93 247 93 00; www.auditori.com; information desk daily 8am–10pm, box office Mon–Sat noon–9pm and Sun 1hr prior to performances; closed Aug), home to the city's resident orchestra, the Orquestra Simfònica de Barcelona (OBC), with a 2,500-seat symphonic hall and a smaller, more intimate space for chamber music. There is also a decent café, see ⑪③.

The Auditori is home to the excellent **Museu de la Música** (tel: 93 256 36 50; www.museumusica.bcn.cat; Mon, Wed–Fri 11am–9pm, Sat, Sun 10am–7pm; charge). It has instruments from all over the world, with an audio guide so that you can hear what they sound like, and it also gives a comprehensive account of how Western music developed. At the end is a room with an electric guitar, cello and harp, which adults and children are invited to play.

Teatre Nacional de Catalunya

Beside the Auditori is the vast Neo-classical National Theatre, the **Teatre Nacional de Catalunya** ❾ (TNC; box office tel: 902 10 12 12; www.tnc.es), designed by Ricardo Bofill and opened in 1998. Plays are generally performed in Catalan, so dance productions may be more accessible to visitors.

Glorìes Flea Market

At the top of Avinguda Meridiana is **Plaça de les Glòries Catalanes** ❿, an elaborate traffic junction that the architect of the Eixample *(see p.66)* originally hoped would become the new city centre. In the middle of the junction, there is even a park.

One exit leads to the **Els Encants** (Mon, Wed, Fri, Sat 8.30am–7pm), a huge flea market, though not really a place for genuine bargains. (Better shopping opportunities may be available at the nearby **Centre Commercial Barcelona Glòries**.)

Torre Agbar

Towering over the area is the lipstick-shaped **Torre Agbar**, designed by the French architect Jean Nouvel, named after the water company **Ag**uas de **Bar**celona and opened in 2005. Known locally as the Suppository, the 144-m (472-ft) building is Barcelona's third tallest, and features a glass façade that glows in shifting hues of red and blue at night, thanks to 4,000 LED lights – inspired, according to Nouvel, by Gaudí.

Above from far left: Aquarama dolphin show; taking a break in the park; L'Auditori; Torre Agbar.

Food and Drink

② L'HIVERNACLE
Parc de la Ciutadella; tel: 93 295 40 17; €€
The park's 1884 hothouse, designed by Josep Amorgòs, is an elegant place to eat and attracts a cool crowd. It is very appealing when it hosts live music – note it stays open after the park shuts.

③ BAR LANTERNA
L'Auditori, Avinguda Meridiana; tel: 93 247 93 00; €
There aren't many obvious places to eat and drink around the Auditori and Teatre Nacional, but the Auditori does have this bar-café serving sandwiches and snacks.

ALONG THE BEACH

Imported golden sand, which is cleaned daily, extends up the coast from Barceloneta, past the Port Olímpic to Poble Nou, Diagonal Mar, the Forum and the Besòs river. It is ideal for a lengthy stroll.

Wintery Walks
Don't automatically discount this route if you visit outside the peak summer months, as the waterfront is a great place for a stroll year-round. In fact, there is something especially satisfying about tucking into a warming alfresco paella lunch after, or part way, through a bracing winter walk.

DISTANCE 7km (4 miles)
TIME 3 hours
START Platja de Sant Sebastià
END Forum
POINTS TO NOTE
In summer, this walk is best done in the morning or late afternoon, when the sun is not too strong. Sant Sebastià, the beach closest to the centre of the Old Town, catches the last of the day's sun, so an option is to do the walk in the opposite direction, ending in Barceloneta.

The curving waterfront strip covered on this route is one of the major legacies of the 1992 Barcelona Olympics. Prior to the regeneration, this was an industrial area, characterised by smoking factories and shunting yards and in steady decline; only the foolhardy ventured onto the beach for a dip in the sea.

The whole area was planned as a smart new residential quarter, with 2,000 apartments in six-storey blocks covering 63ha (160 acres), and initially used as the Vila Olímpica to accommodate the competing athletes.

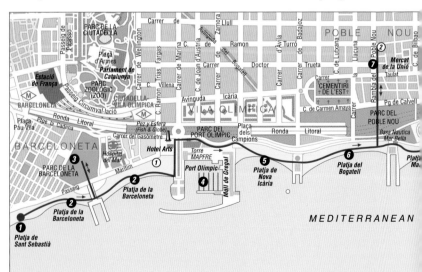

THE BEACHES

There are eight sections of beach along this coast, all well served with showers, bars, Creu Roja (Red Cross) emergency posts and imaginative seats from where you can catch the sun and contemplate the Mediterranean Sea. The main railway line along the coast, serving Estació de França, is buried beneath the Ronda Litoral, which divides the beach from the buildings behind, giving the whole seafront an open, airy aspect. The promenade is popular with joggers, skaters, cyclists and walkers all year round.

Barceloneta Beaches

The walk starts with the 2-km (1¼-mile) **Platja de Sant Sebastià ❶** and **Platja de la Barceloneta ❷** by the fishermen's quarter *(see p.57)*. Before

the regeneration, this was where *xiringuítos* (shack-like beach cafés) drew Barcelonans each summer evening and at weekends, where they would eat fresh fish and sift the sand through their toes. Closest to the city centre, these busy beaches still attract the crowds, and have good facilities.

Just to the north-east of Barceloneta is the **Parc de la Barceloneta ❸**, with the skeleton of an old gasometer, a Modernista warehouse, and a water tower by the Modernista architect Domènech i Estapà.

Contrasting with these are the modern buildings of the Hospital del Mar, one of the city's main hospitals, with a prime site on the waterfront. Its buildings include the innovative horseshoe-shaped Biomedical Research Park (PRBB), covered in wooden slats by Manel Brullet and Albert de Pineda.

Above from far left: busy beach; lifeguard; sandy cycle ride; canoes, ready for a paddle.

Below: beach shots.

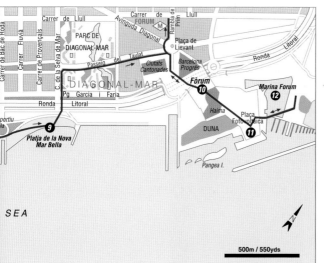

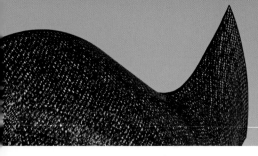

Industrial Past
Can Jaumeandreu (Rambla del Poble Nou 152–60) is a good example of an industrial site put to new use. Known as 'El Vapor de la Llana' (Steaming Fleece), the building, which is distinguished by its lofty octagonal chimney, is now being used as a business centre.

Below: Rambla del Mar, in Poble Nou.

By the hospital, just before the Port Olímpic, walk down to the lower, beach level of the promenade, where there are several bars with sofas. **Bestial**, see ⑪①, is one of the coolest, with 'insects' crawling over its glass entrance.

Port Olímpic
From anywhere on the beach, the **Port Olímpic ④** (Olympic Port) is a beacon, pinpointed by Spain's tallest building, the Hotel Arts *(see p.117)*, designed by Bruce Graham (architect of Chicago's Sears Tower and Hancock Building) and by its neighbour, the MAPFRE building, housing offices. Beside them is a giant, glinting, woven-copper fish, *Pez*

y Esfera (Fish and Sphere) by the architect Frank Gehry, best known for the Bilbao Guggenheim.

The port they overlook was built purely for leisure. Each of its quays is named after a specific wind – *mestral*, *xaloc* and *gregal* (Mistral, West Wind and North-East Wind). Yachts and dinghies set off from the quays, watched by diners in the concentration of restaurants peppered over two levels. Craft stalls are also set out here at weekends.

Beyond the Port
Paella is a speciality of the beach restaurants alongside **Platja de Nova Icària ⑤**, the next stretch of beach. Behind them is the Parc del Port Olimpic, a memento to the Olympics. In Plaça dels Campions (Champion Square) are the names of the 257 gold medallists, as well as the handprints of the footballer Pele, cyclist Eddie Merx, chess champion Gary Kasparov and other sporting stars.

At this point look out for La Font del Cobi (Cobi Fountain), with a statue of the Olympic mascot, Cobi, designed by Xavier Mariscal, one of the first artists to find studio space among the old warehouses here.

The next strip of beach is **Platja del Bogatell ⑥**, hidden from the upper promenade by embankments. The walk here could also be rewarded by a lunch at Xiringuíto Escribà *(see p.122)*.

POBLE NOU

Just before the Mar Bella yacht club, a line of metal poles leads inland to the

Rambla del Poble Nou **❼**, a good place for a lunch or pit-stop. Try a refreshing, tiger-nut *orxata* or an ice cream at **El Tio Che**, see ①②, on the corner of Carrer del Joncar.

Poble Nou used to be known for textile production, and though no factories remain, several fashion designers, such as Josep Font, now have their headquarters here. Gentrification of the area is underway, although not without protests from locals who are concerned that the heart will be knocked out of their community.

DIAGONAL MAR

Back on the beach is **Platja de la Mar Bella ❽**, with a sports centre behind, and the Oca Mar restaurant *(see p.122)* on the jetty that divides it from **Platja de la Nova Mar Bella ❾**.

Here, a new Barcelona is evident. This is **Diagonal Mar**, a new residential and commercial area that has finally brought the great Diagonal avenue that slices diagonally, just as its name describes, through the Eixample, down to the coast.

The focus of the area is **Fòrum ❿**, a cultural centre designed by architects Herzog and de Meuron for a symposium in 2004. An expensive building, with an auditorium and exhibition hall, it has yet to find a true purpose.

Head now to **Plaça Fotovoltaica ⓫**, the location of a football-pitch-sized sun-catcher, with a startling skewed roof of solar panels. The indoor and outdoor auditoria are both spectacular venues for concerts.

A last stop before catching the metro or a tram (line 4) at El Maresme/Forum back to the city centre is the **Marina Forum ⓬**, the latest harbour on this burgeoning leisure coast.

Above from left:
Frank Gehry's woven-copper *Pez y Esfera*; beach loungers; reflection of the Hotel Arts in the MAPFRE building; the Forum.

Just for Joggers
The Passeig Maritim is ideal for joggers. On the far side of Port Olimpic markers are posted for a 1.5-km (1-mile) jog.

Food and Drink 🍴

① BESTIAL
Carrer de Ramon Trias i Fargas 2–4; tel: 93 224 04 07; €€
A trendy place with a multi-level beach-side terrace. Minimal decor and fine Italian-inspired rice and pasta.

② EL TIO CHE
Rambla del Poble Nou 43; tel: 93 268 84 87; €
Founded in 1912 and here since 1933, this bar has the city's best ice creams, plus refreshing lemon slush and deliciously rich *orxata*.

Street Furniture

Among the most striking aspects of this city of *diseny* (design) is the carefully conceived street furniture that makes living outdoors so much more compelling. The tradition is strong. There are 1,600 public drinking fountains in the city, some designed to look like the famous Canaletes on La Rambla *(see p.30)*, but the new ones around the Forum are elegant modern solutions – single corrugated sheets of metal from which water can be drawn. Seating, too, is imaginative. In the centre of the city, there is usually somewhere to sit, with single seats laid out as if in a domestic setting. Around Diagonal Mar new seats are arranged in pairs and threes beneath lamps, like sofas in a drawing room, giving the seafront a sociable air.

THE EIXAMPLE

The showcase for Gaudí and the Modernista architects, the Eixample was laid out on a strict grid traversed by wide avenues. Today the fantastic façades compete for attention with the stylish designer shops and chic locals.

DISTANCE 2km (1½ miles)
TIME 3 hours
START/END Passeig de Gràcia
POINTS TO NOTE

Expect queues at Gaudí's Casa Amatller and La Pedrera – book online for both or try to get there early. Note that from the end of this walk, the Sagrada Família *(see pp.70–1)* is about 15 minutes' walk

The Eixample (Extension) was laid out in 1860 in a grid designed by Ildefons Cerdà i Sunyer. Each block had distinct 'cut-off' corners, which offered great opportunity for a newly rich bourgeoisie to build showy homes. It is part of the city where there is the greatest concentration of buildings designed for domestic purposes by Antoni Gaudí and the Modernistas *(see pp.20–1)*, who shared the belief in craftsmanship and the importance of

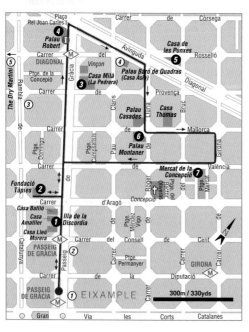

detail, employing masons, ceramicists, stained-glass specialists and workers in bronze and iron to transform their outlandish designs into a reality.

ILLA DE LA DISCORDIA

The tour starts at the Passeig de Gràcia metro. Note that if you need to refuel before heading off, there are some good tapas bars on this broad avenue, see ⑪① and ⑪②. Rambla de Catalunya, west of and parallel to Gràcia, is also very civilized, with pavement cafés and bars including **La Bodegueta**, see ⑪③.

Unmissable on the western side of Passeig de Gràcia, between Carrer del Consell de Cent and Carrer d'Aragó at nos 35–43, is a trilogy of diverse Modernista works, known as **Illa de la Discordia ❶** (Island of Discord), each of which is striking in its own way.

Casa Lleó Morera

On the southern corner of the block, at no. 35, is the privately owned **Casa Lleó Morera** (closed to the public), by Lluís Domènech i Montaner, the architect most renowned for his Palau de la Música Catalana *(see p.44)*. The name comes from the words for 'lions' and 'mulberry trees', both elements used in the decoration. The building is distinguished by its fanciful ovoid towers.

Casa Amatller

Domènech i Montaner mentored Josep Puig i Cadafalch (1867–1957), architect of the next building in the trio: the Dutch-gabled, tiled **Casa Amatller**,

three houses further on, at no. 41. The ground-floor entrance is open to visitors, and there is a bookshop and information point here too. A photography exhibition shows how the house looked when occupied by the Amatller family (a chocolate-making dynasty) after its completion in 1900.

Casa Batlló

Next door, at Passeig de Gràcia 43, is Antoni Gaudí's **Casa Batlló** (daily 9am–8pm; tel: 93 216 03 06; www.casabatllo.es; allow 20 mins queuing time; best to book on-line; charge), with a spectacular blue-green ceramic façade, sensuously curving windows and scale-like roof reminiscent of a sea monster (some suggest that it depicts St George, patron saint of Barcelona, and the dragon). The house was built for textile baron Josep Batlló, from 1902 to 1906, and its apartments, attic and roof are all now open to visitors.

Above from far left: on the roof of the Casa Battló; Casa Amatller; stylish local in the Eixample; colourful Modernista architecture, inspired by nature.
Opposite: rooftop highlights, La Pedrera.
Opposite below: Casa Battló by night.

Modernista Route Purchase a copy of the *Ruta del Modernisme* guide in Casa Amatller or any tourist outlet for the low-down to all 115 identified Modernista sites in the city and beyond, including restaurants and bars, with discount vouchers for entry. See: www.rutadel modernisme.com for further details.

Food and Drink

① BA-BA REEBA
Passeig de Gràcia 28; tel: 93 225 81 88; €€€
Set within a large, two-storey space, this excellent tapas bar-restaurant has a fun modern feel. The kitchen is open from noon to 1.30am.

② TAPA TAPA
Passeig de Gràcia 44; tel: 93 488 33 69; €€
More than 80 different tapas are available in this gastronomic wonder house that is handy for dropping in on any time of day. Good beers, too.

③ LA BODEGUETA
Rambla de Catalunya 100; tel: 93 215 48 94; €€
Old-fashioned bodega with big barrels and marble tables. The rough red wine can be helped down with olives, *tacos de manchego* and *jamón serrano*.

Above from left:
Gaudí's Modernista
hallway, tiles, window
and rooftop 'witch-
scarers', all at
La Pedrera.

Antoni Tàpies
Tàpies, probably
Spain's best-known
living artist, was born
in Barcelona in 1923.
He was a friend
of Joan Miró and
became identified
with a separate
Catalan culture
through his work,
which is abstract
and uncompromising.

FUNDACIÓ TÀPIES

After the Island of Discord, turn left into Carrer d'Aragó. At no. 255, on the northern side of the street and crowned by a twisted metal sculpture entitled *Núvol i Cadira* (Cloud and Chair), is the **Fundació Tàpies ❷** (tel: 93 487 03 15; www.fundaciotapies.org; Tue–Sun 10am–8pm; charge). Established in 1984 by the artist Antoni Tàpies (1923–), the foundation is part gallery – showing work by Tàpies and also temporary exhibitions – and part study centre, with a smart library. It is housed within a building designed by Lluís Domènech i Montaner for his brother's publishing company; built in 1880 it was the first domestic construction in the city to employ an iron frame.

LA PEDRERA

At this point head back down Carrer d'Aragó to the Passeig de Gràcia. Cross the road and walk up to no. 92, by the corner of Carrer de Provença, and **Casa**

Milà ❸ (tel: 902 400 973; www.caixa catalunya.es; daily 10am–8pm; charge), more commonly referred to as 'La Pedrera', meaning 'the stone quarry', after its rippling grey stone façade.

Begun in 1901, this extraordinary edifice – Gaudí's most prominent private building – was a controversial project: an eight-storey apartment block devoid of straight lines, set around two inner courtyards. Gaudí put the city's first underground carriage park in the basement and sculpted a roof of evil-looking chimneys that were dubbed *espantabruixes*, or 'witch-scarers', inspired by Medieval knights.

After years of falling into decay the building was rescued when Unesco declared it of world-heritage importance, and the Caixa de Catalunya savings bank undertook its restoration. The courtyard, attic (housing an exhibition on Gaudí's work, and of note for its fine parabolic arches), rooftop decorated with *trencadis* (mosaic of broken tiles) and show flat, in which everything is carefully designed in the Modernista

Below: La Pedrera

style, can all be visited. There is also a separate exhibition space for changing temporary shows on the first floor.

North of the Pedrera

Just beyond La Pedrera, at Passeig de Gràcia 96, is **Vinçon**, a leading interior design store, selling everything from stylish stationery and retro toys to furniture and fabrics; exhibitions are also held here. Go upstairs to appreciate the building, which was once the home of the artist Ramón Casas (1866–1932).

Just nearby, at Plaça del Rei Joan Carles I, is **Palau Robert ❹**, home to an information centre for Catalonia. Exhibitions are also held here, and there is also a pleasant peaceful garden.

AVINGUDA DIAGONAL

Turn right, onto Avinguda Diagonal, which cuts the Eixample diagonally and runs down to the sea. On the right, at no. 373, is the **Palau Baró de Quadras**, built in 1904 by Puig i Cadafalch and now home to **Casa Àsia** (tel: 93 238 73 37; www.casaasia.es; Mon–Sat 10am–8pm, Sun 10am–2pm; free) a cultural centre focusing on Asia and the Asian Pacific through exhibitions and its library. There is a beautiful small courtyard, lovely glass balconies on the second floor, a café, see ④, and rooftop terrace.

As you continue heading down the Diagonal, look out, two blocks along, for Puig i Cadafalch's Neo-Gothic **Casa de les Punxes ❺** (House of the Spikes). The apartment block is officially called the Casa Terrades but is nicknamed after its spiky towers.

Modernista Landmarks

At this point turn right down Carrer de Roger de Llúria. At the corner of Carrer de Mallorca, on the northern side, is the **Palau Casades**, now housing by the Il.lustre Col.legi d'Advocats (Law College). On the south side is **Palau Montaner ❻** (Sat–Sun 10am–2pm; charge) with attractive tiled eaves and a mosaic exterior. Designed by Domènech i Montaner as a private home for his publisher brother – the whole family lived here from 1893 until 1939 – it now shelters the government of Madrid in Barcelona.

Domènech i Montaner also built **Casa Thomas** at Carrer de Mallorca, 291–3, a few steps down on the left, and now occupied by **El Favorita**, a modern furniture designers. (You can walk in and admire the building.)

Continue a block to Carrer de Girona, then turn right and right again to reach the 19th-century glass-and-iron **Mercat de la Concepció ❼** (Carrer d'Aragó 313–17; tel: 93 457 53 29; www.laconcepcio.com; Mon 8am–3pm, Tue–Fri 8am–8pm, Sat 8am–4pm; see p.14), selling all manner of foodstuffs and with a couple of bar-style stalls where you can get a drink and a snack. To return to Passeig de Gràcia from here, simply walk west along Carrer de València.

Fashion Tips

Some of Barcelona's key designers are based in the Eixample. One of the best known is Antonio Miró, whose main shop is at Carrer del Consell de Cent 349. Josep Font is at Carrer de Provença 30. Other places to visit include Bad Habits at Carrer de València, 261, the outlet for Mireya Ruiz, with experimental textures, forms and fabrics. In the same street (no. 273) is On Land, with clothes for both men and women from young designers including Josep Abri. Also worth a look is Camiseria Pons, attractively located in a Modernista building at Carrer Gran de Gràcia 49.

Food and Drink 🍴

④ BAR AZAFRÁN
Casa Àsia, 373 Avinguda Diagonal; tel: 93 238 73 37; €
On the ground floor of the Asian centre is this attractive café-bar, which does a range of Oriental-style drinks and snacks.

SAGRADA FAMILIA AND PARK GÜELL

No visit to Barcelona is complete without a tour of the buildings of the great Modernista architect Antoni Gaudí. His stunning Sagrada Família is an essential visit, and can be combined with a trip to Gaudí's house-museum in the fantasy-style Park Güell, nesting high above the city.

DISTANCE 3km (2 miles)

TIME 4-hours

START Sagrada Família

END Park Güell

POINTS TO NOTE

This is a two-destination tour, and you can buy a combined ticket for both the Sagrada Familia and the Casa-Museu Gaudi in Park Güell at either place.

Start the day with the astonishing, unfinished temple of Antoni Gaudí (1852–1926), easily reached by metro (Sagrada Família station on lines L2 and L5). If you are hungry during the tour, try one of the outlets on Avinguda de Gaudí, see ⑪①.

SAGRADA FAMÍLIA

After Gaudí had completed his last commission, Casa Milà (La Pedrera; *see p.68),* in 1910, he devoted the remaining 16 years of his life to the **Temple Expiatori de la Sagrada Família ❶** (Carrer de Mallorca 401; tel: 93 207 30 31; www.sagradafamilia.org; Mar–Sept: daily 9am–8pm, Oct–Feb: daily 9am–6pm; charge; guided tours available; combined ticket option to Park Güell, valid for one month). Gaudí spent his last 10 years working unpaid from a hut

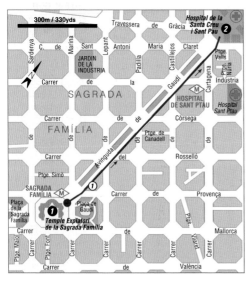

Food and Drink 🍴

① LA RENAIXENÇA

Avinguda de Gaudí 16; tel: 93 347 67 40; €

There are a lot of fast-food outlets around the Sagrada Família, especially on Avinguda de Gaudí. This pizzeria is a good standby.

on site. He lived extremely modestly, putting all his money and energy into his building, until his death in 1926.

Existing Façades

Before entering, it is worth circling the yet unfinished building to get an idea of its layout. The austere west front was completed in the 1980s with statues by a local artist, Josep Maria Subirachs, and by the Japanese sculptor, Etsuro Soto. The only façade Gaudí completed himself is the eastern one dedicated to the Nativity, with three doorways to Faith, Hope and Charity, and four coloured, tentacled towers, one of which has an internal lift to take vertigo-free visitors skywards.

Work in Progress

Part of the fascination lies in watching the builders and craftsmen going about their work – both high up in the air and on the ground, in the wall-less nave, where plans are also displayed. At 110m (360ft) in length, the Sagrada Família will eventually be 27m (87ft) longer than the city's cathedral and nearly twice the height, with a main tower rising to 198m (650ft), half as high again as those that are already here. Completion is currently set for around 25 to 30 years' time – the once preferred date of 2026, commemorating the centenary of Gaudí's death now looking increasingly unlikely. However, mass will be held in the church from 2008.

Crypt

The crypt where Gaudí is buried also houses the museum that shows how he envisaged the finished temple, and how his ideas often changed. A scale model reveals how the pillars in the nave, which for a long time has served as a builder's yard, will be like an avenue of trees in an enchanted wood.

HOSPITAL DE LA SANTA CREU

On leaving the Sagrada Família, look – or stroll – up Avinguda de Gaudí on the north side of the temple. This anarchic diagonal avenue – Gaudí disliked the rigidity of the Eixample – leads to the **Hospital de la Santa Creu i Sant Pau** ❷ (Carrer de Sant Antoni María Claret 167; tel: 93 291 90 00; www.santpau.es; free).

Designed by Lluís Domènech i Montaner, and begun in 1902, the hospital is a fine Modernista work, with separate pavilions connected by underground walkways, in the style of a pleasant garden city to speed the recovery of its patients. The building is set at a 45 degree angle to the rest of the Eixample, so that it catches the sun better. It is now a Unesco World Heritage Site.

PARK GÜELL

At this point, it is time to progress to **Park Güell** ❸ (Carrer d'Olot; daily 10am–sunset; free). There are several ways of reaching it from the Sagrada Família: hop on the tourist bus outside the church; take the metro to Lesseps (*as shown on map*), then walk (uphill) 1,200m (³⁄₄ mile) or take the no. 24

Above from far left: view of the Sagrada Família from across the city at Montjüic (*see p.73*), showing a diver in the 1992 Olympic Games; the church's eastern façade, which was finished by Gaudí; spire detail; a work in progress.

Opposite and below: details from the Sagrada Família and Park Güell.

Above from left:
Casa-Museu Gaudí;
mosaic sculpture;
Montjuïc's Caixa-
Forum; Fundació
Joan Miró.

Park Plots
Only three plots for
Güell's planned
garden city were
sold. One was
bought by Gaudí
himself and is now
the Casa-Museu; the
other two were sold
to the Trias family,
who still own them.

bus; or take the no. 92 bus from outside the Hospital de la Santa Creu i Sant Pau. Alternatively, simply hail a taxi.

Background

The site was originally owned by Gaudí's patron, the affluent industrialist Eusebi Güell, who had wanted to create a garden city of houses here – hence the English spelling of 'park'. The project never came to full fruition, and in 1922 the Güell family donated the park to the city instead.

The Park

The main entrance is flanked by two whimsical pavilions designed by Gaudí. The one on the left is a shop, while the one on the right houses an exhibition giving the background to the construction of the park.

500m / 550yds
PARC DEL CARMEL
PARK GÜELL
3 · Casa-Museu Gaudí
LESSEPS

A double staircase, presided over by a magnificent tile-mosaic salamander *(see p.10)*, leads up to the park's main feature, a two-tiered plaza. The lower part is a hypostyle hall, originally intended to be the market hall for the estate. Framing the plaza is a wavy, tile-mosaic parapet from where there is a grand view out over the city. This long, colourful, undulating bench *(see p.21)* – which, with the salamander, is the most photographed aspect of the park – was actually the work not of Gaudí but of his assistant, Josep Jujol i Gibert.

Take time to wander the pathways that wind through the park. Some are in the form of extraordinary viaducts supported by twisting stone pillars. Green parakeets can often be spotted darting in and out of the palm trees.

Casa-Museu Gaudí

In 1906, Gaudí bought the home of architect Francesc Berenguer, a short distance into the park, to the right of the entrance. The sweet building, which is like something out of a fairytale, is now the **Casa-Museu Gaudí** (tel: 93 219 38 11; Apr–Sept: daily 10am–7.45pm, Oct–Mar: daily 10am–5.45pm; charge). On three floors, it still houses furniture from the architect's time here, including his bed, *prie-dieu* and crucifix, as well as furniture brought from elsewhere.

Return to the centre on bus 24 or 25, or from Lesseps metro. If you are still feeling energetic, you could walk down to Gràcia *(see pp.82–3)* from here, for a look at Gaudí's Casa Vicens.

MONTJUÏC

Named after a Jewish cemetery, Barcelona's southern hill is home to the region's most notable art collection, a scattering of buildings erected for the 1992 Olympics, the world-class Fundació Joan Miró and the fun Poble Espanyol.

The buildings that were erected for the 1992 Olympic Games were the last in a line of attractions to be located on the 213-m (700-ft) high hill of Montjuïc. The majority of the grand exhibition halls and cultural palaces here are remnants of the city's previous key cultural event, the Universal Exhibition of 1929.

But the hill has long featured in the city's history. Its stone was quarried to build the cathedral, and its castle, which has a wonderful 360-degree panorama, has witnessed all the triumphs and cruelties of the city's history *(see pp.24–5)*.

To see everything on Montjuïc would take more than a day, and this tour concentrates on its main sites, while mentioning those along the way, so you can pick and choose what you would like to see.

PLAÇA D'ESPANYA

The best way to approach Montjuïc, to fully appreciate its grandeur, is from the **Plaça d'Espanya ❶**, served by metro lines 1 and 3. Beside the square is the Neo-Mudéjar **Las Arenas**, a vast bullring built in 1899 in the North African style. The ring is not used for bullfights, since these are banned in Catalonia by the Generalitat (local government).

DISTANCE 5km (3 miles)

TIME 5 hours

START Plaça d'Espanya

END Paral.lel metro

POINTS TO NOTE

You will not be able to do justice to all Montjuïc's attractions in a day, so decide which elements you want to see before setting out. The hill is steep and the roads meander; take the bus or funicalr *(see right)*, to save energy.

UP TOWARDS THE HILL

From here walk up **Avinguda de la Reina Maria Cristina** through Lluís Domènech i Montaner's copies of Venice's campanile, which flagged the triumphant approach to the 1929 exhibition. On either side of this esplanade are the vast trade fair halls of Barcelona's **Fira de Barcelona**, some of which have been doing useful service ever since 1929.

Font Màgica de Montjuïc

At the top of the avenue, reached by outdoor escalators (if they are working), is the **Font Màgica de Montjuïc ❷** (Magic Fountain; tel: 93 316 10 00; www.bcn.es/fonts; May–Sept: Thur–Sun 8pm–midnight, Oct–May: Fri–Sat 7–9pm; free), designed by Carles Buïgas

No Bullfighting

The Generalitat (local authority) is officially opposed to bullfighting.

Funicular and Bus

One way of getting up and down Montjuïc is to use the funicular that runs from Paral.lel metro to just above the Fundació Joan Miró. From there the teleféric cable car ascends to the castle. The hop-on, hop-off tourist bus from Plaça d'Espanya to the castle runs every 40 minutes from mid-June to mid-September (weekends only in winter), stopping at all the major sights mentioned in this route on the way. Alternatively, hop in a taxi to take you from sight to sight.

Above from left:
Pavelló Mies van der
Rohe; statue at the
pavilion; decorative
dome at the Palau
Nacional; exterior of
the Palau Nacional.

'Barcelona' Chair
Mies van der Rohe
designed his now-
iconic chrome-and-
leather 'Barcelona'
chair as a throne for
the Spanish king
and queen on their
visit to the 1929
Universal Exhibition.

in 1929. Rising to 50m (164ft), it is particularly magnificent in the evenings,
when it is lit by over 4,500 coloured
lights and dances to music from
Beethoven to Hollywood theme tunes.

Museu d'Arqueologia and Around

If you were to head left at this point,
you would soon reach the **Mercat de
les Flors**, a complex of theatres that
includes the **Institut del Teatre** and
Teatre Lliure, which puts on a broad
range of stage productions, and has a
good restaurant, see ⑪①.

Nearby is the **Museu d'Arqueologia**
(Passeig de Santa Madrona 39–41; tel:
93 423 21 49; www.mac.es; Tue–Sat
9.30am–7pm, Sun 10am–2.30pm;
charge). Constructed for the 1929 exhibition as the Palace of Graphic Arts, the
museum houses archaeological finds

from the city, from the Graeco-Roman
trading post at Empúries and from the
Iberian settlement at Ullastret on the
Costa Brava.

Opposite the museum is a public
garden leading to the open-air **Teatre
Grec**. Also built for the 1929 exhibition and set in a former stone quarry,
it is used for plays and concerts in the
summer, as part of the two-month
Festival del Grec (tel: 93 316 10 00;
www.bcn.es/grec).

Pavelló Mies van der Rohe

Back at the Font Màgica, just to its
right, on Avinguda del Marquès de
Comillas, is the **Pavelló Mies van der
Rohe** (Mies van der Rohe Pavilion;
tel: 93 423 40 16; daily 10am–8pm;
charge). It was designed by Bauhaus
director Mies van der Rohe as the

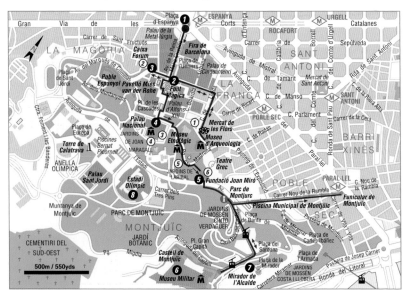

German Pavilion, a reception area for the 1929 exhibition, and is remarkable for its spare lines in sleek marble and glass, complemented by a tranquil small pool. The original pavilion was demolished after the Universal Exhibition, but it was rebuilt in 1986 to celebrate the centenary of the designer's birth.

CaixaForum

Opposite the pavilion is a Modernista factory, Casaramona, built in 1911 by Josep Puig i Cadafalch. Redesigned by Arata Isozaki as the **CaixaForum** ❸ (Avinguda del Marquès de Comillas 6–8; tel: 93 476 86 00; www.fundacio.lacaixa.es; Tue–Sun 10am–8pm; free), it is one of the most exciting cultural spaces in the city, staging exhibitions across its four galleries, plus concerts, films and talks. It is also home to a media centre and a bookshop, and a good café, see ⑪②.

PALAU NACIONAL

The next main sight en route is the **Palau Nacional** ❹, the formidable neoclassical palace that dominates the fountain and the approach up Avinguda de la Reina Cristina. The palace is home to the **Museu Nacional d'Art de Catalunya** (MNAC; tel: 93 622 03 76; www.mnac.es; Tue–Sat 10am–7pm, Sun 10am–2.30pm; charge except first Thur of month; tickets are valid for two days), a repository of Catalan, Renaissance, Gothic and modern art, and, most notably, the finest collection of Romanesque art in the world.

Food and Drink

① **EL LLIURE**
Teatre Lliure, Passeig Santa Madrona; tel: 93 325 00 75; €€
This theatre restaurant is open before performances until 1am and at lunch (Tue–Sat 1–4pm). An innovative menu for indoor and outdoor dining.

② **LAIE-CAIXAFORUM**
Avinguda del Marquès de Comillas 6–8; tel: 93 476 86 69; €
The restaurant in the CaixaForum offers a daily set menu, plus a wide choice of salads, sandwiches, pastries and juices.

Poble Espanyol

If you continue walking up Avinguda del Marquès de Comillas from the CaixaForum, you will reach the Poble Espanyol or Spanish Village (tel: 93 325 78 66; www.poble-espanyol.com; 9am till late; charge), one of the city's most popular sites, attracting 1.5 million, mostly Spanish, visitors a year. Some 120 buildings represent architecture from across Spain, from Moorish Andalusia to the rugged Basque country, in styles from the 12th to the 19th centuries. The complex was designed for the 1929 exhibition and has since become a leisure centre and the 'City of Artisans', where you can see glassmakers, weavers, potters and ironmongers at work. Its restaurants are popular in the evenings, and night spots include the Tablao de Carmen, with a flamenco show, and a hip club, La Terraza, with open-air dancing in summer. The whole complex is enclosed within a replica of the walls of the city of Àvila, and one of the towers, the Torres de Àvila, is also a popular club.

Above from left:
Fundació Joan Miró;
Immaculada Con-
cepció by Francisco
de Zurbarán, at
the MNAC; Torre de
Calatrava; cable cars.

The Collection

The most striking of its lower rooms devoted to Romanesque decoration are those containing wall paintings peeled from the apses of remote Pyrenean churches in the early 20th century, transported here by mule train and restored. These are complemented by crucifixes, altarpieces and caskets.

The collection of Gothic and Renaissance art on the upper floors is less complete, though Catalonia's Gothic masters Jaume Huguet, Bernat Martorell and Lluís Dalman are represented. The Baroque assemblage has been enhanced by the addition of the Thyssen collection that was formerly housed in the Pedralbes monastery *(see p.80)*.

The museum's Catalan collection includes 19th- and 20th-century work by Casas, Rusiñol, Nonell and Fortuny, as well as decorative art from Modernista interiors, including furniture by Gaudí and Jujol. One room has nine works by Picasso; another is dedicated to Catalan photography, with a small collection of prints including a couple of iconic pictures from the Civil War.

In addition to the galleries, the museum also houses a large concert hall, an open-plan area with comfortable sofas on the first floor beneath the building's dome, a café, see ⑪③, and a smarter restaurant, **Oleum**, see ⑪④.

FUNDACIÓ JOAN MIRÓ

The next suggested main stop on the route is the Fundació Joan Miró, which can be reached by turning right out of the Palau Nacional and walking up the hill. This takes you past the **Museu Etnològic** (Passeig de Santa Madrona; tel: 93 424 68 07; www.museuetnologic.bcn.es; summer: Tue–Sat noon–8pm, winter: Tue, Thur 10am–7pm, Wed, Fri–Sun 10am–2pm; charge), the city's recently renovated Ethnology Museum. Turn into the lovely **Jardins de Laribal** (10am–sunset; free), where the **El Font del Gat** café-restaurant, see ⑪⑤, makes for a pleasant pitstop.

A short walk further is the **Fundació Joan Miró ❺** (Miró Foundation; tel: 93 329 19 08; www.bcn.fjmiro.es; Oct–June: Tue–Sat 10am–7pm, July–Sept: Tue–Sat 10am–8pm, year-round: Thur till 9.30pm, Sun 10am–2.30pm; charge), in a building by

Montjuïc's Gardens

There are a number of gardens on Montjuïc – the formal, French-style Jardins de Joan Maragall form the grounds of the Palauet Albéniz, while the Jardins de Mossèn Cinto Verdaguer are in the English country-house style. The recently opened 14-ha (35-acre) Jardí Botànic, between the Olympic Stadium and the castle, is a sustainable garden showcasing plants from across the Mediterranean. Jardins de Mossèn Costa i Llobrera, on the south side of the hill and sloping towards the sea, was once a strategic defence point for the city, the Buenavista battery. This

is now a cactus garden, one of the best gardens in the world according to *The New York Times*. It has cacti from across Mexico, Bolivia, Africa and California. A 5-star hotel is to be built here, as part of the plans to further redevelop Montjuïc.

architect Josep Lluís Sert (1902–83) to showcase the work of the painter Joan Miró (1893–1983) and opened in 1975. The two, who were friends, were both from Barcelona, but lived most of their lives in exile from the Franco regime: Miró in Paris then Mallorca; Sert in the US, where he became head of the architecture faculty at Harvard.

The gallery houses a large and excellent collection of Miró's work, including his trademark primary-colour sculptures out on the roof. Concerts are held here regularly, and there is also a pleasant restaurant, see ⑪⑥.

CASTELL DE MONTJUÏC

From the gallery, walk five minutes up Avinguda de Mirimar to the **Funicular station**. Opposite is the Montjuïc **tourist information** centre. From here, you can either take the Telefèric cable car or a bus for the five-minute ride up to the **Castell de Montjuïc ❻**. Built in 1640 during the Harvesters' Revolt the castle was redesigned in the reign of Felipe V. In 1939, at the end of the Civil War, it was used as a prison and execution ground. Nowadays, it houses the **Museu Militar** (tel: 93 329 86 13; Tue–Sun 9.30am–8pm; till 5pm in winter; charge). Exhibits in its cavernous halls include an assortment of weaponry, miniature soldiers, flags, uniforms and paintings and other items of memorabilia.

From just below the castle, by the **Mirador de l'Alcalde ❼** and the statue of Sardana dancers, the Telefèric will take you back to the Funicular and Paral.lel metro, or you can get a bus back to Plaça d'Espanya.

OLYMPIC SIGHTS

If you want to admire the legacy of the 1992 Olympic Games, take the bus that runs between the castle and the Plaça d'Espanya, and get off at the **Estadi Olímpic ❽** (Olympic Stadium) stop. What you see today is the remodelled 1929 stadium, with a permanent exhibition of the 1992 event in the **Galeria Olímpica** (Mon–Fri 10am–1pm, 4–6pm; free).

Just beyond it are the striking **Palau Sant Jordi** indoor sports stadium and the **Bernat Picornell** swimming pool. The 188-m (616-ft) **Torre de Calatrava** communications tower rises from the **Plaça d'Europa**, from where there are fine views to the south.

High Divers

Up the road from the funicular station are the municipal baths, the Piscines Bernat Picornell (Avinguda de l'Estadi 30–40; tel: 93 423 40 41; www.picornell.com; outdoor pool: June–Sept: Mon–Sat 9am–9pm, Sun 9am–8pm, Oct–May: Mon–Sat 10am–7pm, Sun 10am–4pm; indoor pool longer hours; charge). They were built for the diving events in the 1992 Olympics. With precipitous tiered seating, they have fabulous views of the city (see p.70). In high summer, films are sometimes shown here in the evenings, from 10pm.

Food and Drink 🍴

③ CUBIC CAFETERIA
Palau Nacional; tel: 93 622 03 60; €
A slice of of the Oval Hall is taken up with this straightforward café, which serves sandwiches and pastries.

④ OLEUM
Palau Nacional; tel: 93 289 06 79; €€
With its panorama views reflected in its mirrored ceiling, this smart restaurant serves Mediterranean cuisine from 1pm to 4pm.

⑤ EL FONT DEL GAT
Passeig de Santa Madrona 28; tel: 93 289 04 04; closed Tue; €€
In the middle of the formal gardens, this café-restaurant was built by Puig i Cadalach. It does excellent, innovative food with home-made ices and sorbets, and a good fixed-price menu at lunch.

⑥ BAR RESTAURANT
Fundació Miró, Avinguda de Miramar 1; tel: 93 329 07 68; €
Lovely restaurant with an outdoor courtyard and good staples such as pasta plus local dishes including an aromatic rabbit stew.

BARÇA

One of the world's richest football clubs, with about 100,000 members, and Barcelona's top team, Barça infuses the city with pride. Its museum, the focus of this short tour, is one of the most popular in the city.

DISTANCE 1km (½ mile)

TIME 2 hours

START/END Palau Reial metro

POINTS TO NOTE

This is a good family outing: it is relatively brief, with just a short walk to the stadium from the metro, and not expensive. It could be combined with a visit to Palau Reial *(see p.81)*.

More than a Club

The Barça slogan, *'més que un club'* (more than a club), reflects the club's place in the cultural history of Catalonia. It presents Barça as the defender of rights and freedoms, a reputation earned during the Franco years, when matches against Madrid were notoriously weighted in the capital's favour. Today, Barça's fan base extends well beyond Catalonia, and to show its continued caring side towards the world, it makes a regular contribution to United Nations' humanitarian aid programmes, and players wear the Unicef logo on their shirts.

After the Museu Picasso *(see p.47)*, the museum at Barça football club is the most visited in the city. Fans from all over the world come to see one of Europe's largest stadiums, to wonder at the club's many trophies, watch playbacks, gloat over past glories and stand in the directors' box.

Barça matches bring the city to a standstill and have Barcelonans in thrall (note that the city does have another football club, Espanyol, who are based at the Estadi Olímpic on Montjuïc; *see p.77*).

Getting There

When you step out of the **Palau Reial metro ❶** on the south side of Avinguda Diagonal, the dome of the stadium is immediately evident behind the massive university car park. It is just a 10-minute walk through the car park to the entrance, where stalls sell souvenir scarves, strips and other memorabilia. But wait till you get inside the wire fence to find the largest collection of memorabilia in the two-storey **FCBotiga Megastore**. Next to it is a café, see ⑪①.

CAMP NOU STADIUM

The stadium, **Camp Nou ❷** (Avinguda de Aristides Maillol, Les Corts;

tel: 93 496 36 00; www.fcbarcelona.com; Mon–Sat 10am–6.30pm, Sun 10am–2pm; charge), meaning 'new camp', has been home to the club since 1957. It is the largest constituent part of a sports complex just below the university campus and the smart end of Avinguda Diagonal and can hold around 110,000 spectators.

Basketball, hockey, handball, junior football and ice hockey are also catered for in its neighbouring buildings, the **Mini Estadi**, the **Palau Blaugrana** (*blau* translates as blue, *grana* as burgundy: the club colours) and the **Pista de Gel** ice rink.

Tour and Museum

The main ticket office, opposite the store, is where to buy tickets to the **Museu del FC Barcelona** (opening hours as above). The entrance fee includes a 45-minute tour of the dressing rooms, tunnel to the pitch, players' benches, presidential box and press room. The museum contains the many trophies Barça has amassed in its long, illustrious history, during which the team has become synonymous with Catalan aspirations. There is a roll-call of famous players and managers, and action-replay videos. The best part, however, is simply looking out on to the breathtaking arena and imagining the mood during games.

Food and Drink 🍴

① SANDWICHES & FRIENDS

Camp Nou; opposite ticket office; €
This efficient, friendly chain has an outlet in the grounds right beside the souvenir shop, with outside tables and a relaxed family atmosphere.

Above from far left: inside Barça football club; supportive flags.

Above: Barça badge; club scarves.

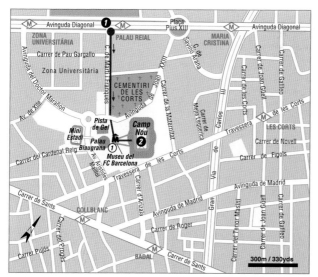

Ticket Sales

Match tickets go on sale on weekdays, from 9am to 1pm and 4 to 8pm. Same-day tickets can be bought in the stadium's ticket offices on Travessera de les Corts or Avinguda de Joan XXIII. Matches start between 5 and 9pm. *Entrada general* are cheap, top-tier tickets, *Lateral* are mid-priced ones, and *Tribuna* are for covered seats. Note that tickets are scarce for big matches.

PEDRALBES

This tour starts in the genteel suburb of Sarrià, then heads to the atmospheric Gothic monastery of Pedralbes in the hills and, further down, the 20th-century Palau Reial, which has a fabulous ceramics collection.

DISTANCE 2km (1 mile)

TIME 3 hours

START Reina Elisenda FGC station, Sarrià

END Palau Reial metro

POINTS TO NOTE

The FGC train from Plaça de Catalunya takes 10 mins to Sarrià (bus from Catalunya takes 40 mins), from where it is a 10-min walk to the monastery, then 20 mins on foot to the Palau Reial. Take a bottle of water with you, as there are few cafés en route.

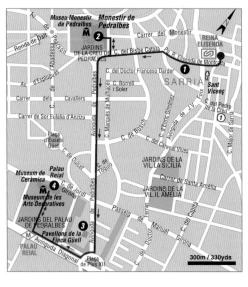

Reina Elisenda FGC station is in the centre of **Sarrià ❶**, once a village, now a atmospheric, sought-after district of Barcelona, with a market, smoky bars and traditional restaurants, see ⑪①. The *barrio* is somewhat reminiscent of a provincial Catalan town with gardens bursting with bougainvillea, pretty Modernista villas and old-fashioned shops.

THE MONASTERY

From the station, it is a 10-minute walk along Passeig de la Reina Elisenda de Montcada to the gold-stoned **Monestir de Pedralbes ❷** (Baixada del Monestir 9; tel: 93 203 92 82; Apr–Sept: Tue–Sat 10am–5pm, Oct–Mar: Tue–Sat 10am–2pm; all year: Sun 10am–3pm; charge except first Sun of month), accessed up a cobbled lane and through an arch.

The monastery was founded by Queen Elisenda de Montcada, wife of Jaume II (the Just), for nuns of the Order of St Clare. The queen took the vows and retreated here after Jaume's death in 1327. There are still a few nuns living here, but most parts of the monastery are open to visitors as the **Museu Monestir de Pedralbes**.

The three-storey cloister is Catalan-Gothic at its most elegant. In the gardens are fruit trees, and former nuns' cells lead off around the sides. The most

beautifully decorated cell, painted in 1346 by the Catalan painter Ferrer Bassa (who studied under Giotto), belonged to the queen's niece. There are numerous treasures on display, mostly paintings and religious artefacts.

When the monastery was fully operational, the sick were tended in the infirmary, and four rooms from this part of the complex now contain exhibits on the daily routine of the Poor Clares who lived here. You can visit the refectory where they ate in silence and, beside it, the kitchens, which are blue-tiled with stone sinks.

The Church

Leaving the museum, continue up the side of the building to reach the entrance to the complex's church, a simple Gothic building containing Queen Elisenda's marble tomb. Part of the nave at the back of the church, behind a grille, is used by the few nuns who live in the buildings opposite the old monastery.

FINCA GÜELL

Leave the monastery and walk down Avinguda de Pedralbes for about 10 minutes, past the luxurious (but rather soulless) apartment blocks in this exclusive part of town. Near the bottom, on the former farm estate of Gaudí's patron, Eusabi Güell, you will see, at no. 7, the **Pavellons de la Finca Güell** ❸ (tel: 93 317 76 52; www.rutadel modernisme.com; open for guided visits only; tours in English Fri–Mon 10.15am and 12.15pm; charge) with a magnificent entrance gate, a tortuous

iron work by Gaudí featuring a dragon known as the Drac de Pedralbes. One pavilion houses a Ruta del Modernisme *(see p.67)* information centre.

PALAU REIAL

Beyond the Finca, accessed from Avinguda Diagonal, the Renaissance-style **Palau Reial** ❹ (Avinguda Palau Reial de Pedralbes), surrounded by formal Italianate gardens, was built by the city council in 1925 to encourage visits from Alfonso XIII. The king went into exile six years later, but his throne room is still here.

Decorative Arts Museums

The palace now houses two museums, the **Museu de Ceràmica** and **Museu de les Arts Decoratives** (tel: 93 280 16 21; www.museuceramica.bcn.es; www.museuartsdecoratives.bcn.es; Tue–Sat 10am–6pm, Sun 10am–3pm; charge except first Sun of month). The ceramics collection includes Islamic tiles, pottery by Picasso and modern works, while the decorative arts museum showcases items from Renaissance furniture and painted bridal trunks to 20th-century design.

Return to the city centre via the Palau Reial metro, situated just outside the palace entrance.

Above from far left: frescoes by Ferrer Bassa; cross at the monastery; statue at the Palau Reial; monastery cloisters.

Above: details from the Museu de les Arts Decoratives.

Food and Drink 🍴

① CASA JOANA
Carrer Major de Sarrià 59, Sarrià; tel: 93 203 10 36; €
Long-established, little-changed place, serving tasty home cooking at good prices. Popular with local families at weekends.

GRÀCIA

Away from the bustle of the town centre, the slightly bohemian neighbourhood of Gràcia offers peaceful streets, some with lovely Modernista façades, intriguing shops and bars, and a sense of community.

DISTANCE 2km (1 mile)

TIME 1hr 30mins

START Fontana metro

END Diagonal metro

POINTS TO NOTE

This is a suggested walk around Gràcia, but there are few key monuments in this area. For ease of walking, the tour starts at the top and goes downhill.

Above: fashions *(top)* and accessories *(centre)* at Valentino; sculpture in Plaça del Sol.

The Time of Doves

Plaça del Diament is the setting for Mercè Rodoreda's 1962 novel of the same name (*The Time of Doves* in English). The book has been translated into more languages than any other Catalan work of literature.

Above the Diagonal, beyond the Passeig de Gràcia, the *vila* of Gràcia was, until 1897, a community in its own right. With a reputation for radicalism and a strong identity, it maintains a tradition of artisans and small family businesses. It is full of lovely cafés and bars and attractive little squares.

By day the small shops, boutiques and alternative outlets have a charming, quirky, feel, but by night, as doors open on bars, restaurants and a couple of small cinemas, as well as a theatre with a strong local reputation, the area has a more vibrant ambience.

CASA VICENS

Start at the **Fontana metro ❶** in **Carrer Gran de Gràcia**, an extension of the Passeig de Gràcia, lined with shops and Modernista apartment blocks and also the location of one of Barcelona's finest fish restaurants, the Galician **Botafumeiro**, see ⑪①. The Modernista façades are even more striking in **Rambla del Prat** (left out of the station, then first right).

At the end of the Rambla turn right, then take the second right down Carrer de les Carolines, and you will see **Casa Vicens ❷**, on the left. This was Antoni Gaudí's first major commission, attained at the age of 32, from a ceramic and tile

manufacturer – as is evident from the colourful façade. Note the highly elaborate fence *(see pp.100–1)*. Closed to the public, the building has been inhabited by the same family since its completion in 1885.

PLAÇA DEL SOL

Continue across Gran de Gràcia, turn right and zigzag down the small streets, lined with workshops, groceries and trendy clothes shops, until you reach **Plaça del Sol ❸**. A favourite spot among students and young people as well as local families, it is lined by cafés, including the ever-popular **Sol Soler**, see ⑪②.

As the evening wears on, the families take their children home, and the square becomes a centre of the area's night-time buzz. Attractive architecture includes the green *esgrafiat* (incised decoration) on the Envalira restaurant, while a Lebanese restaurant in the square is a sign of the growing social mix.

PLAÇA DE RIUS I TAULET

Continue down, across the lively Travessera de Gràcia, home to the area's market, to **Plaça de Rius i Taulet ❹**, Gràcia's main square. Highlights here include **El Rellotge**, the 1864 town hall clock tower that sees in Barcelona's New Year on television each year. Like all Gràcia squares, this is a popular place for people to sit and children to play.

Wend your way towards the bottom of Gran de Gràcia and **Casa Fuster ❺** *(see below)*. From here it is just a short walk down to Avinguda Diagonal and the Diagonal metro.

Above from far left:
Casa Vicens; taking a stroll in Gràcia.

Festa Major
For a whole week around 15 August Gràcia's streets and squares are filled with music, parades, cava drinkers and wildly innovative designs, as the residents compete for the title of best decorated street.

Casa Fuster

At the bottom of Carrer Gran de Gràcia is Casa Fuster, Domènech i Montaner's last building in Barcelona, completed in 1911. Built over six storeys with marble columns and luxuriant stone carving, it was at the time described as the most expensive private building in the city. For many years the Café Vienès occupied the ground floor, and the El Danubio dance hall, a focal point for society, was in the basement. In 2000 the building was purchased by the Hoteles Center company and overhauled as a magnificent 5-star hotel, and the Café Vienès *(illustrated below)* reopened on the ground floor.

16 TIBIDABO

The hill that looks down on Barcelona is crowned by an old-fashioned amusement park and criss-crossed by walking paths. It is accessible by tram and funicular, with the excellent CosmoCaixa science museum en route.

DISTANCE 10km (6 miles)
TIME 5 hours
START Avinguda Tibidabo FGC
END Plaça de Catalunya
POINTS TO NOTE

Tibidabo funfair is open from Easter to December only. The best time to visit is late afternoon or early evening, as the sunsets are spectacular. The Tramvia Blau and funicular only run when the Parc d'Atraccions is open.

Above: stained-glass window in the Sagrat Cor; friendly Tramvia Blau.

According to the Bible, the Devil took Christ up into 'an exceeding high mountain and sheweth him all the kingdoms of the world, and the glory of them; and saith unto him, All these things *I will give thee* [*tibi dabo*] if thou wilt fall down and worship me.'

Tibidabo is the 517-m (1,700-ft) summit of the Collserola hills that hang behind the city. With the haze caused by city traffic there is usually a fine view of the skyline only, but on rare occasions the view reaches across

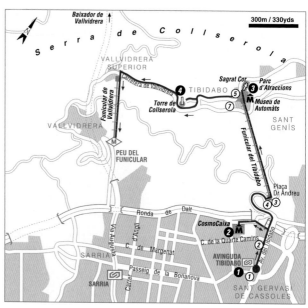

Barcelona to the sea, the Balearic Islands, north to the Pyrenees and west to Montserrat.

An afternoon or evening out at these dizzy heights can be a family occasion, starting with hands-on fun at Cosmo-Caixa, Barcelona's science museum, before continuing up the hill to take in the Tibidabo amusement park.

TRAMVIA BLAU

Getting up the hill is part of the fun. Take the FGC train to **Avinguda Tibidabo** ❶ station, fortify yourself with a hot chocolate at **El Forn de San Salvador**, see ⑪①, then cross over Passeig de Sant Gervasi. Here, at the beginning of Avinguda del Tibidabo, is the stop for the old-fashioned, open-sided wooden **Tramvia Blau** (Blue Tram) that will take you to the funicular that goes up to Tibidabo every 30 minutes. The more-frequent no. 195 bus, which leaves from the stop a few steps further on, also goes to the fun park.

Avinguda del Tibidabo

The ride up this grand avenue takes you past Modernista houses and villas, built for the city's elite intent on escaping the hassle of industrial Barcelona, and characterised by lavish turrets and tiles. The villa at no. 31 is now the smart **El Asador de Aranda**, see ⑪②.

COSMOCAIXA

Part way up the hill, en route to the funicular (about 15 minutes' walk or two stops on bus no. 60) is the science museum, **CosmoCaixa** ❷ (Carrer de Teodor Roviralta 47–51; tel: 93 212 60 50; www.fundacio.la caixa.es; Tue–Sun 10am–8pm; charge). Situated on the left just before the Ronda de Dalt highway, it is one of the most entertaining museums in the city.

There are a large number of interactive exhibits, including energy and force machines, and computers to test your reflexes, equilibrium, colour awareness and ability to lie. There are also microscopes and satellite pictures and even a submarine. Click de Nens, an area aimed at 3- to 6-year-olds, was created by designer Xavier Mariscal to give little ones their first taste of science, through stimulating interactive displays.

When you have finished at the museum, continue up the hill towards the funicular. (Return to the bus stop, to head up that way, if you can't face the walk.)

Above from far left: looking down from Tibidabo; inside CosmoCaixa science museum; admiring the views; the exterior of CosmoCaixa.

CosmoCaixa
Be warned that the entrance fee to the science museum is higher than that for most Barcelona museums. This reflects the wear and tear that the interactive machines suffer from parties of eager schoolchildren.

Food and Drink 🍴

① EL FORN DE SAN SALVADOR
Carrer de Balmes 445; no tel; €€
This small café by the Avinguda Tibidabo station exit serves *xocolata desfeta*, nourishing hot chocolate, thick enough to stand a spoon in.

② EL ASADOR DE ARANDA
Avinguda del Tibidabo 31; tel: 93 417 01 15; €€€
The flagship of this high-quality chain of restaurants, El Asador de Aranda serves typically Castilian hearty food. The house speciality is lamb roasted in a clay oven.

Above from left:
toy museum;
Madonna depicted in
stained glass at the
Sagrat Cor; the big
wheel; Viking ride.

High Flyer
The red aeroplane
ride (Avion Tibiair) at
Tibidabo was made
in 1928, and the
plane is a replica of
the first one to fly
between Madrid
and Barcelona.

Drinks with a View

Once across the Ronda de Dalt, the road
winds through bosky estates peppered
with Modernist fantasies of arcaded terraces and grand portals until it reaches
the funicular station at Plaça del Doctor
Andreu. Here, there is a choice of places
to stop for a drink with great views over
the city, including **La Venta**, see ⑪③,
and **Mirablau**, see ⑪④.

The Funicular

The Art Deco funicular, which opened
in 1901, runs regularly up to the top of
Tibidabo, taking seven minutes to
ascend its almost-vertical track. You
should choose at the outset whether to
buy a single or return ticket (a return
is slightly cheaper than two singles).
If you fancy a 30-minute bus ride back
to Plaça de Catalunya from the top –
or a walk down – plump for a single.

PARC D'ATRACCIONS

The **Parc d'Atraccions** ❸ (Plaça del
Tibidabo; tel: 93 211 79 42; www.
tibidabo.es; Mar, Apr: Sat, Sun noon–
8pm, June: Sat, Sun noon–9pm, July:
Wed–Fri noon–9pm, Sat noon–11pm,
Sun noon–10pm, Aug: Mon–Thur
noon–10pm, Fri–Sun noon–11pm,
Sept: Sat, Sun noon–9pm, Oct: Sat
noon–9pm, Sun noon–8pm, Nov–mid-
Dec, mid-Jan–Feb: Sat, Sun noon–
6pm; all-in tickets permit unlimited
access to the rides; cheaper tickets for
just six rides are also available).

The amusements are fairly tame: cars
drifting gingerly out across the hill, a
big wheel and helter-skelter. The
Pasaje de Terror (Passage of Terror)
and Avion Tibiair, a red aeroplane that
swoops off the side of the hill, are
probably the only rides that will turn

Food and Drink 🍴

③ LA VENTA
Plaça del Doctor Andreu s/n; tel: 93 212 64 55; €€€
Stylish bar and restaurant offering Catalan dishes.

④ MIRABLAU
Plaça del Doctor Andreu 2; tel: 93 418 58 79; €€€
An elegant cocktail lounge with a restaurant upstairs. Used as a
nightclub in the evening.

⑤ RESTAURANT LA MASIA
Plaça del Tibidabo 3–4; tel: 93 417 63 50; €€
Sandwiches and snacks are served on the outdoor terrace of
Hotel La Masia. Inside is a popular restaurant.

⑥ GRAN HOTEL LA FLORIDA
Carretera de Vallvidrera al Tibidabo 83–93; tel: 93 259 30 00; €€€€
Opened in 1925, this grand venue has now been revitalised.
You can eat at L'Orangerie, the lovely restaurant, or just drop
in for a drink at the bar.

knuckles white. There is also a **Museu de Automàts**, with mechanical toys from the first half of the 20th century.

THE SAGRAT COR

There is more to Tibidabo than the funfair, however. There are restaurants on the hill with panoramic views, including **La Masia** and the **Gran Hotel La Florida**, see ⑪⑤ and ⑪⑥, and pleasant paths to walk. Many visitors come here just to visit the **Sagrat Cor** (Plaça del Tibidabo tel: 93 417 56 96; daily 10am–2pm, 3–7pm; charge), the Sacred Heart church, a bulky 20th-century architectural confection on the site of a chapel used by the hermit, then saint, Joan Bosco, in the 19th century. There is a lift in the tower up to the top of the church from where there are marvellous views of the city. The original chapel can still be seen behind the main church.

TORRE DE COLLSEROLA

At this point you may wish to return to the city either the way you came or by bus from Plaça del Tibidabo.

But if you are up for an even more spectacular view, head off down the road behind the Hotel La Masia to the prominent **Torre de Collserola** ❹ (Centra de Vallvidrera al Tibidabo; tel: 93 406 93 54; www.torrecollserola. com; Wed–Sat 11am–2.30pm, 3.30–8pm; charge), which you will undoubtedly have seen ever since your arrival on Tibidabo. You can take the lift to the glassed-in observation platform on

the 10th floor of the 288-m (945-ft) communications tower. Designed by British architect Norman Foster for the 1992 Olympics, it is sometimes known as **Torre Foster**.

If you wanted to return a different way you could walk on for another 20 minutes or so, to reach the Modernista Funicular station of **Vallvidrera Superior**. The Funicular takes you down to the FGC station at **Peu del Funicular**, from where it is only a 15-minute train ride back to Plaça de Catalunya.

Model Pilots

Members of the Club Vellers Collserola turn out on the hills most evenings in summer to fly their model planes and they organise around 10 competitions a year. The models have wingspans of up to 5m (15ft).

The Collserola Hills

The Collserola park, on the other side of the hill from the funfair, is a great place for walks, cycling or picnics. A mere 13-minute train ride from Plaça de Catalunya through a tunnel takes you to Baixador de Vallvidrera. Here you step out into another world, with the pine-scented air hitting you as soon as the doors open. Walk up the landscaped path to the Centre d'Informació del Parc de Collserola (9.30am–3pm): a helpful base, with an exhibition on local wildlife, maps, advice and a bar/restaurant. Close to it is the atmospheric Villa Joana (Sat–Sun 11am–3pm; free), where the much-loved poet Jacint Verdaguer lived until his death in 1902. Footpaths lead into the woods with *fonts* (natural springs) and picnic spots. To explore further, take the funicular from Peu del Funicular to Vallvidrera and get off halfway up at Carretera de les Aigües, a track that is popular with joggers, cyclists, ramblers and model-plane makers.

SITGES

Just 40km (25 miles) south of Barcelona and generally sunnier, the elegant seaside town of Sitges has a rich artistic heritage, having long attracted painters, writers and other creatives. Since the 1960s, it has been the focal point of the gay scene on this stretch of coastal north-eastern Spain.

Above: beach slides; prawns fresh from the sea.

DISTANCE 40km (25 miles) one way

TIME A full day

STAR Sitges train station

END Cementiri de Sant Sebastia

POINTS TO NOTE

Regular trains to Sitges run from Passeig de Gràcia or Sants stations (line C2), taking around 40 mins. By car, the C32 motorway has been blasted through the Garraf mountains to alleviate the congested autovia (motorway) that winds along by the sea south from Barcelona. Whatever your method of arrival, do not forget to bring your swimming costume.

American Route

The Sitges tourist office (Carrer Pintor Morera 1; tel: 93 894 42 51; www.sitges tur.com; July–Sept: daily 9am–8pm, Oct–June 9am–2pm, 4–6.30pm) offers an 'Americanos Route' tour that takes in the villas and mansions built by Sitges' sons and daughters who returned from their prosperous ventures in the Americas.

Food and Drink

① REVES

Carrer de Sant Fransesc 35; tel: 93 894 76 25; €€

Attractive restaurant/tapas bar near the station. Tasty menu featuring the local speciality *xató de sitges* (beans with clams) and other seafood.

② BAR XATET

Carrer de Sant Francesc 1; tel: 93 894 74 71; €€

The town's oldest bar/café dates from 1925; hams hang from the ceiling like stalactites, so fill up with a sandwich or a plate of the cold cuts.

The best known of the coastal resorts within easy reach of Barcelona, Sitges is an attractive, cosmopolitan place with excellent shops, great restaurants and a buzzing gay scene.

The Making of a Resort

A former wine town that had trade links with America, Sitges prospered in the 19th century, when so-called *americanos*, locals who had found fortune abroad, came home to retire in mansions and build summer houses.

The Luminist School of Sitges, comprising artists such as Joan Roig i Soler and Arcadi Mas i Fontdevila, were attracted by the superior quality of light in this seaside town in the second half of the 19th century. However, when *fin-de-siècle* Modernista artist and writer Santiago Rusiñol (1861–1931) bought a home here in 1891, Sitges was dubbed 'the Mecca of Modernisme' by the Barcelona press, and Rusiñol was credited with having discovered the place.

The resort's popularity with the bohemian crowd continued: Spanish poet and playwright Federico García Lorca (1899–1936) stayed here, as did the French composer Erik Satie (1866–1925) and the English writer G.K. Chesterton (1874–1936).

In the late 1950s and early 1960s Sitges responded to the flood of tourists to the coast with pubs, bars and a few hotels; locals rented out rooms in summer, and a few entrepreneurs built modest apartment blocks here. It was at this point that the town became a magnet for the gay community.

TOWARDS THE OLD TOWN

As you exit from **Sitges station** ❶ you will pass the municipal **Mercat** (Mon–Thur 8am–2pm, Fri–Sat 8am–2pm and 5.30–8.30pm). If you want to eat while you are in the vicinity of the station, two recommendations for food are the restaurant **Reves**, see ⑪①, and **Bar Xatet**, see ⑪②.

From the station, all roads seem to lead down to the sea. The first three cross Carrer de Sant Gaudenci and lead to **Plaça Cap de La Villa** ❷, the heart of the pedestrianised shopping area, with numerous cafés and bars spilling on to the street.

Left of here, on Carrer d'Angel Vidal, is the **Pati Blau**, a recreation of a painting of a blue courtyard by Rusiñol. Straight ahead is Carrer Major, which takes you down to the old town.

MUSEU ROMÀNTIC

At this point, however, our recommendation is a detour to the right down Carrer de Parallades, a busy shopping street, then first right into Carrer de Sant Guadenci for the **Museu Romàntic** ❸ (Casa Llopis, Carrer de Sant Gaudenci 1; tel: 93 894 29 69; summer: Tue–Sat 9.30am–2pm and 4–7pm, Sun

Above from far left: view of the rooftops of Sitges; the town's busy beach.

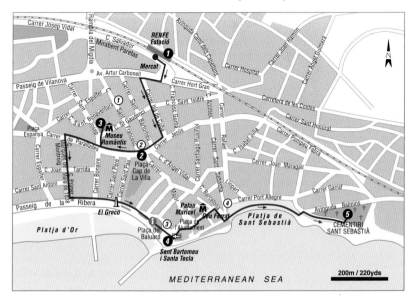

Above from left: tiled frieze; view of the town from the beach.

10am–3pm; winter: Tue–Sat 9.30am–2pm and 3.30–6.30pm; Sun 10am–3pm; guided tours on the hour also include entrance to the town's other main museums, with the same opening times; charge). This house, built in 1793 by the cultured Llopis family, was given in its entirety to the town as a museum of family life. On the top floor is a large collection of antique dolls amassed by local children's writer Lola Anglada (1893–1984).

CARRER DEL PECAT

Continue down Carrer de Parallades to Carrer del Marqués de Montroig and Carrer Primer de Maig de 1838 – the date, 1 May, commemorates an attack on the liberal town by reactionary Carlists. This is the main pedestrian avenue running down to the sea, lined with bars and sun-seekers at café tables, and popularly known as the Street of Sin, **Carrer del Pecat**.

This is the focal point for some of the largest events in Sitges' busy festive calendar. At Corpus Christi (in May or June), the street is covered in a carpet of flowers, while during the pre-Lent carnival parade, there is an elaborate show of costume and design here. The Shrove Tuesday evening parade is probably the town's most outrageous spectacle, with the glamour hitting top notes at the transvestite festival, complete with glitzy costumes.

THE BEACH

At the bottom of the street is the palm-fringed promenade Passeig de la Ribera, which is lined by the gently curving **Platja d'Or**, a golden strand some 5km (3 miles) long. If you are hungry at this point and would like an upmarket lunch, continue to the left, towards the end of the beach promenade for **Fragata**, see ⑪③.

PALAU MARICEL

The beach ends just beyond the monument to the painter El Greco on the rocky promontory dominated by the 17th-century church of **Sant Bartomeu i Santa Tecla ❹**.

Just behind the church, in Carrer Fonollar, are some magnificent white mansions and, on the left at nos 2–6, the **Palau Maricel** (tel: 93 811 33 11; tours Tue 8pm and Thur 10pm; booking essential; charge), with a lovely blue-tiled roof terrace. The palace was built in 1910 by the American philanthropist Charles Deering (1852–1927) to house his art collection (sadly now dispersed). Concerts are sometimes held here.

Xató
Fried fish and squid dishes are popular in seaside Sitges, but a local speciality is *xató*, a salad of escarole (a variety of endive), tuna, dried cod and anchovy, with a dressing that may include nuts and peppers.

Food and Drink 🍴

③ FRAGATA
Passeig de la Ribera 1; tel: 93 894 10 86; €€€€
Situated among a cluster of restaurants at the end of the promenade near the church of Sant Bartolomeu i Santa Tecla, this unfussy restaurant serves up top-notch seafood specialities, with meat dishes, too.

④ LA TORRETA
Carrer Port Alegre 1; tel: 93 894 5253; €€€€
On a quieter stretch of the seafront, this is a traditional Sitges seafood restaurant, with rice dishes, and a good place to try *xató (see above)*.

Deering also purchased the building opposite, a former hospital dating from the 14th century, and connected it to his own palace by an overhead passageway. The hospital now houses the **Museu Maricel** (Carrer Fonollar; tel: 93 894 03 64; summer: Tue–Sat 9.30am–2pm and 4–7pm, Sun 10am–3pm, winter: Tue–Sat 9.30am–2pm and 3.30–6.30pm; Sun 10am–3pm; charge), with a fine collection of Gothic paintings and furniture and a room decorated by Josep Luís Sert. This is also the home of the town's main art collection, with works by the Romantics, Luminists and Modernistas who were associated with Sitges; a portrait of Deering by Ramon Casas is among them.

SANTIAGO RUSIÑOL

The neighbouring building is home to the **Museu Cau Ferrat** (Carrer Fonollar; tel: 93 894 03 64; summer: Tue–Sat 9.30am–2pm and 4–7pm, Sun 10am–3pm, winter: Tue–Sat 9.30am–2pm and 3.30–6.30pm, Sun 10am–3pm; charge), erstwhile home of the painter Santiago Rusiñol and now the showcase to his collection, including two El Grecos (bought in Paris, they were carried through the town, with a statue of the artist, in a mock Holy Week procession), five small Picassos and works by Casas.

Like many artists of his generation, Rusiñol was funded by his family, which had grown rich thanks to Barcelona's industrial revolution. Rusiñol travelled frequently to Paris, forging important links for local artists. He purchased fishermen's cottages in Sitges, which he converted into a mansion to house his collection of ironwork, sculptures and paintings and to use as a studio. Between 1892 and 1899 he also organised the Festes Modernistes, a music and drama festival.

SANT SEBASTIÀ BEACH

North of these imposing buildings is **Platja de Sant Sebastià**. Quieter than the main beach, it offers good restaurants, including **La Torreta**, see ⑪④, and pavement cafés.

If it is not too hot, or if you tire of the beach, an option is to head up the scrubby paths on the far side of Platja de Sant Sebastià towards to the atmospheric **Cementiri de Sant Sebastià** ❺ (Avinguda Balmins; tel: 93 811 20 81; summer: Mon–Sat 8am–1pm, 3–5pm, Sun 9am–1pm, winter: Mon–Sat 9am–1pm, 3–6pm, Sun 9am–1pm; 1 Nov: 8am–6pm; free), the town's cemetery.

Below: detail of Santiago Rusiñol's *Morphine* (1894).

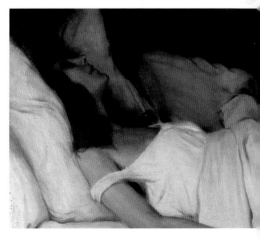

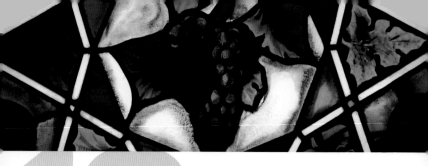

WINE TOUR

Catalonia is a major wine-producing region, known for its cava. A tour of the Penedès region gives you a chance to see some lovely countryside as well as tasting various delicious wines.

Seaside Drive

If you have a hire car, a trip through the Penedès vineyards could be combined with a visit to Sitges (see pp.88–91). If you don't have a car, there are travel agencies and tour operators that organise wine and gastronomy tours from Barcelona. The most comprehensive information on visits to some 300 wine and cava producers can be found at the Vilafranca Tourist Office (Carrer Cort 14; tel: 93 818 12 54; www.turisme vilafranca.com).

DISTANCE 55km (35 miles)
TIME A full day
START Sant Sadurní d'Anoia
END Vilafranca
POINTS TO NOTE

To reach the starting point from Barcelona take the train from Sants or Plaça de Catalunya; they leave every hour and take 45 mins. To continue the train journey to Vilafranca del Penedès, pick up the same line; Vilafranca is just 10–15 mins further. It you are travelling by car, take the A7 motorway out of Barcelona; this passes both towns. Note that many wineries close in August, and the wine museum is closed on Monday.

Food and Drink 🍴

① CAL TON
Carrer de Casal 8. Vilafranca del Penedès; tel: 93 890 37 41; €€€
Chef Toni Matta has a reputation for innovative modern Catalan cooking using the best of the local ingredients from land and sea.

② CAFÉ EL CORO
Plaça de la Villa; Vilafranca del Penedès; no tel; €
Sit at marble-topped tables and enjoy the simple local fare at this café on Vilafranca's main square.

Catalonia's most significant contribution to the world of wine is cava, an inexpensive, earthy, non-acidic sparkling drink produced in the same way as Champagne, but by law forbidden the French *appellation*. Around 90 per cent of the country's output comes from the Penedès region, south of Barcelona, in vineyards around the town of Sant Sadurní d'Anoia. Catalonia's main wine town is nearby Vilafranca del Penedès.

Visiting both Sant Sadurní and Vilafranca will give you a flavour not just of the product but of the countryside. For details of how to get to Sant Sadurní, see the grey box left.

SANT SADURNÍ D'ANOIA

Freixenet

Beside the station at **Sant Sadurní d'Anoia ❶** is **Freixenet** (Carrer de Joan Sala 2; tel: 93 891 70 00; Mon–Thur 10am–1pm and 3–4.30pm, Fri–Sun 10am–1pm; www. freixenet.es; charge), one of the largest producers in the region. There are regular 90-minute tours of its cellars with tastings and opportunities to buy afterwards.

Codorníu

Even more impressive is the original home of cava, **Codorníu** (Avinguda de Jaume Codorníu; tel: 93 891 33 42;

www.codorniu.com; pre-arranged tours only; charge), about 20 minutes' walk (signposted) from the station. Josep Raventós, of the Codorníu family dynasty, popped the first cava cork here in 1872, and his son Manuel added the huge Modernista cellars designed by Puig i Cadafalch from 1902–15. The cellars are now a national monument. A tour of Codorníu includes an explanation of the wine-making business, a tour of the museum at the winery and a train ride through part of the five storeys of cellars that cover some 26km (16 miles).

VILAFRANCA

Opportunities for lunch in a small country town such as Sant Sadurní are fairly limited, so at this point we recommend continuing to **Vilafranca del Penedès ❷**, slightly further down the train line (also on the A7), instead. There are some excellent restaurants here, including the upmarket **Cal Ton**, see ⑪①️ (note the plaque that indicates that it is on the **Ruta del Vi i del Cava**, the Route of Wine and Cava).

For a more low-key option, try the **Café el Coro**, see ⑪②️, on the Plaça de la Villa. The square is also home to the town hall and a tourist information centre.

Torres

All the bars bear the motto *Hi ha Cava a copes* (There is cava by the glass here), but Vilafranca is actually the centre for still-wine production. The old bodega of the great **Torres** family is at Carrer de Comercio 22, beside the station. You can also visit their state-of-the-art winery at **Pacs** (Mon–Fri 9am–5pm, Sun 9am–1pm; tel: 93 817 74 87; www. torres.es; charge), just outside the town.

Museu del Vi

Spain's best wine museum, the **Museu del Vi** (Plaça de Jaume I 1; tel: 93 890 05 82; June–Aug: Tue–Sat 10am–9pm, Sun 10am–2pm; Sept–May: 10am–2pm, 4–7pm; charge includes tasting) occupies a former royal palace in Plaça de Jaume I, opposite the basilica of Santa Maria. The museum showcases wine-making implements, and a bar displays the region's wine.

Above from far left: stained-glass window at the Museu del Vi in Vilafranca; cellars at Freixenet in Sant Sadurní d'Anoia.

Above: some of the different types of cava produced at Freixenet.

Human Pyramids
Wall tiles in the Plaça de la Villa in Vilafranca celebrate the *castellers*. These human pyramids are attempted at the end of August as teams, physically supported by the crowds, compete for height, balance and skill.

DALÍ TOUR

The Surrealist artist Salvador Dalí was born and lived in the Empordà region, where his museum, home and the castle he gave to his wife Gala – the 'Dalí Triangle' – are worthy legacies of his eccentricity and talent.

Gala

In 1929 Dalí met Russian-born Elena Ivanovna Diakonova (1894–1982), nick-naming her Gala. She had previously been married to the poet Paul Eluard, with whom she had a daughter, and had also had a relation-ship with Max Ernst. She and Dalí married in 1958.

DISTANCE 80km (50 miles)
TIME At least a full day
START Figueres
END Port Lligat or Púbol
POINTS TO NOTE

This route includes three main sights: the Teatre-Museu Dalí in Figueres; Dalí's house in Port Lligat; and the Castell Gala-Dalí at Púbol. The first is accessible by train from Barcelona; the second by bus, but to visit all three sights, you will need to hire a car.

FIGUERES

Salvador Dalí was born in 1904 in the pleasant market town (market day is Thursday) of **Figueres ❶** not far from the French border, and it is here that he found a permanent home for his work at **Teatre-Museu Dalí** (Plaça Gala-Salvador Dalí 5; tel: 972 67 75 00; www.salvador-dali.org/museus/figueres; July–Sept: daily 9am–7.15pm, Oct: 9.30am–5.15pm; Nov–Feb: 10.30am–5.15pm; Mar–June: 9.30am–5.15pm; charge).

The museum, opened in 1974, was built on the site of a theatre that was burned down at the end of the Civil War. The adjacent Torre Galatea (named after his wife, Gala), added in 1981, is where Dalí died in 1989. He is buried in the crypt in the museum's lower level.

The Collection

Among the extraordinary works here are the *Poetry of America, or Cosmic Athletes*, painted in 1943, a portrait of Gala as Leda (the swan), and the huge ceiling fresco dominating the Wind Palace Room on the first floor. In the garden, the *Rainy Cadillac* sculpture is a crowd puller.

A good place to eat in Figueres is the **Hotel Empordà**, see ⑪①.

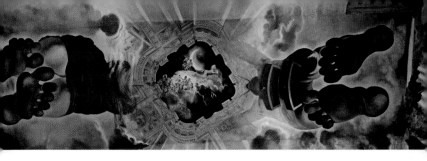

PORT LLIGAT

From Figueres it is around 40km (25 miles) east on the C260 and GI614 to the seaside town of **Cadaqués**.

Casa-Museu Dalí

Located just over the hill, in the next cove, is **Port Lligat ❷** and the seafront **Casa-Museu Dalí** (Port Lligat; tel: 972 25 10 15; www.salvador-dali. org/museus/portlligat; mid-Mar–mid-June, mid-Sept–early Jan: Tue–Sun 10.30am–6pm, mid-June–mid-Sept: daily 9.30am–9pm; booking essential; charge). Dalí and Gala lived for many years in this gorgeous house, actually a collection of fishermen's cottages.

Set in a garden of gnarled olive trees, the house offers insight into the Dalís' domestic life. Huge windows frame views of the fishermen's cove and the Mediterranean, and in the Yellow Room a mirror is angled so that Dalí could see the light of the rising sun while in bed in the open-plan adjoining room.

Gala's touch is visible in many areas, particularly in the Room of the Cupboards, where she covered cupboard doors with photographs and magazine covers, and in the 'everlasting flowers' with which she festooned the windows.

The swimming pool area is an example of Dalían kitsch: modelled on a pool at the Moorish Alhambra in Granada, it is embellished with a statue of Diana the Huntress, models of Michelin men and Pirelli tyres.

If it is time for lunch after your visit, **Hotel Port Lligat**, see ⑪②, is just across the road.

PÚBOL

To continue the tour (only possible if you are travelling by car, as there are poor public transport connections between Port Lligat and Púbol), head back in the direction of Figueres until you see signs for the C31 south to Girona. Continue on this road until you hit the C252, towards Púbol.

Castell Gala-Dalí

The highlight in Púbol is the **Castell Gala-Dalí ❸** (Plaça Gala-Dalí; tel: 972 48 86 55; www.salvador-dali.org/museus/pubol; mid-Mar–mid-June, mid-Sept–early Jan: Tue–Sun 10.30am–6pm, mid-June–mid Sept: daily 9.30am–9pm; charge). Dalí restored this magnificent three-storey Gothic-Renaissance castle and presented it to Gala in 1970, promising only to enter it at her invitation. He painted frescoes in the interior and built the crypt where Gala is buried. On the day of her death in 1982 he moved into it himself and stayed, becoming increasingly frail, until a fire two years later obliged him to move back to the Torre Galatea.

Above from far left: exterior of the Teatre-Museu Dalí in Figueres; spectacular ceiling fresco at the Teatre-Museu Dalí.

Above: the Teatre-Museu, Figueres; the inimitable Salvador Dalí; crowds outside the museum.

Food and Drink 🍴

① HOTEL EMPORDÀ

Antigua Carretera de França s/n; Figueres; tel: 972 50 05 62; €€€
The late chef Josep Mercadé was one of the first cooks to reinvent Catalan dishes, and his inspirational approach is still strongly evident in this unpretentious restaurant in Figueres.

② HOTEL PORT LLIGAT

Carretera de Port Lligat, Port Lligat; tel: 972 25 81 62; €€
This restaurant is in a lovely spot opposite Dalí's house, and the terrace is open for lunch from June to September. The hotel is also a relaxed place to stay if you want to extend your tour of the area.

MONTSERRAT

The Black Virgin, the patron saint of Catalonia, is the revered icon at the heart of this monastery complex, set in stunning scenery on top of the jagged hills just an hour from Barcelona.

Travelling By Train?
There are various ticket options from Barcelona to Montserrat, some of which also cover funicular journeys. You will need to specify which one you want right at the start of the journey, at the station on Plaça d'Espanya.

DISTANCE 100km (60 miles) rtn
TIME A full day, possibly two
START/END Montserrat
POINTS TO NOTE
You can drive or take a train to reach the starting point from Barcelona. FGC trains to Montserrat leave from Plaça d'Espanya. To make the most of the day (and to hear the boys' choir at first sitting) catch the 9.36am train. For an overnight stay, there are two places offering accommodation at the monastery: the Cel.les Abat Marcet apartments and the 3-star Hotel Abat Cisernos (for both tel: 93 877 77 01). Packages, offering guides, are also available; see www.abadiamontserrat. net for details. Take a bottle of water, warm clothing and walking shoes.

The serrated mountain, **Montserrat**, is Barcelona's most holy shrine. Its blunt, grey rocky walls rise to a sheer 1,241m (4,075ft) and extend more than 50 sq km (19 sq miles), making it visible not only from miles around, but also on flights in and out of Barcelona airport.

Although a trip to Montserrat makes a great day out from Barcelona, note that the spectacular views will be hampered on cloudy or overcast days; note also that the weather at this height can be changeable, cold and turbulent, so come prepared with warm clothing.

La Moreneta

Displayed in the 16th-century basilica of the monastic complex is La Moreneta, the Black Virgin of Montserrat – a Romanesque statue of the Madonna

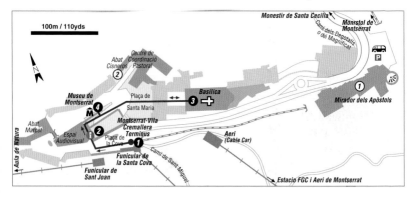

and Child that has long been the subject of great veneration.

Catalans are not especially known for their devoutness, however, and this statue and her mountain have captured their imagination for political as much as for religious reasons. In her rocky stronghold, La Moreneta is looked to for protection against invaders and tyrants, and her elected abbot is seen as an upholder of Catalan liberties.

During the 40-year Franco regime, when the Catalan language was officially forbidden, baptisms and weddings were still held in Catalan here. Catalans are expected to make a pilgrimage to this holy mountain once in their lives, and its choir is renowned the world over.

GETTING THERE

Montserrat lies some 50km (30 miles) inland, 45 minutes by car along the autovia to Martorell. FGC trains run from Plaça d'Espanya every hour (36 minutes past the hour; 6 minutes past for the return journey) on the R5 line (Montserrat–Martorell), and take one hour either to the **Aeri de Montserrat** station, where a cable car takes five minutes to reach the monastery; for a slightly more comfortable journey, continue on the train to the next stop, **Monistrol de Montserrat**, from where a Cremallera rack-and-pinion train takes 15 minutes to head up the mountain to the monastery. (There is a free, patrolled car park at Monistrol station, from where motorists can catch the Cremallera; this is a good option especially at weekends, when

the car park at the monastery itself gets very crowded.) Once out of town, it is not long before the mountains' distinctive peaks come into view.

Montserrat-Vila Cremallera

As you get out of **Montserrat-Vila Cremallera Terminus ❶** (the cable car arrives a little further down) the whole monastery complex and its awe-inspiring rock backdrop come into view. Adjacent to the entrance to the monastery area is an **information office ❷** (tel: 93 835 02 51), where you can watch an engaging audiovisual show entitled *Montserrat Portes Endins* (Inside Montserrat), giving an account of the lives of the Benedictine monks who still reside here, running, among other things, a publishing house and record label for the choir.

THE BASILICA

Steps lead up to the main square and the **Basilica ❸** (8am–10.30am and noon–6.30pm; free). The monastery has been a Benedictine place of prayer since AD 967, but the buildings you see today date from after its most recent destruction, in 1811, by Napoleon's troops, who plundered its treasures and burnt its library. It was more than 50 years before the monks returned, and the basilica was only given its present façade, featuring Christ and his apostles, in 1900.

La Moreneta

A separate door at the front of the basilica leads to the statue of **La Moreneta**, set above the altar. Devo-

Above from far left: the jagged mountains from which the monastery takes its name; in the basilica.

Above: stained glass in the basilica.

Local Produce
Look out for stalls outside the monastery selling delicious locally made honey and cheese.

Above: inside the basilica; religious sculptures; hiking in the hills.

tees can touch the orb clutched in her hand, the only part of the statue not behind glass. White lead used in the painting of her flesh is thought to have oxidised to give her the dark appearance, which was subsequently painted in a matching colour. Legend says that the statue was made by St Luke and brought to Barcelona by St Peter. Royalty and nobility have pledged themselves to her. St Ignatius Loyola, founder of the Jesuits, dedicated himself to her service.

The Choir

The monastery has had a choir school since the 13th century, and one of the highlights inside the basilica is the performance by the angelic-voiced boys' choir, the **Escolania** (Mon–Fri 1pm, 6.45pm, Sun noon and 6.45pm; no choir June 24–mid-Aug and 26 Dec–8 Jan). The choir sings for just 10 minutes, and one of the works generally rendered is *Virolai*, composed in 1888 by the poet-priest Jacinct Verdaguer to mark the millennium of the monastery. Note, however, that if you stay to listen to the evening performance, you will miss the last cable car back to the station.

The Museum

Outside the basilica in the Plaça de Santa Maria is the entrance to the underground **Museu de Montserrat** ❹ (Mon–Fri 10am–6.45pm, Sat–Sun 9.30am–7.45pm; charge), remodelled (along with the square) by Modernista architect Puig i Cadafalch in 1929.

There are five distinct collections in these spacious galleries: the Archaeology of the Bible, with treasures from Egypt, Rome and Byzantium; iconography of Our Lady of Montserrat; church gold and silverware; paintings from the 13th–18th centuries, notably works by El Greco, Tiepolo and Caravaggio; and a 19th- and 20th-century art collection, including minor works by Dalí, Degas, Monet, Picasso and Sisley and the largest collection of the Catalan school outside Barcelona's MNAC *(see p.75)*.

WALKS AND EXCURSIONS

From the monastery, there are a number of set walks, lasting from just 30 minutes to three and a half hours and well signposted, some following long-distance (GR) routes; for details ask at the information office at Cremallera or the nature centre. The scent from herbs and flowers, plus the views and dramatic rock formations made by alluvial

---

Food and Drink 🍴

There are several options at the monastery complex, including a self-service restaurant, a bar, and a picnic area, plus:

① RESTAURANTE MONTSERRAT
Monestir de Montserrat; tel: 93 877 77 01; €€
On the lower floor of the building (which also houses a bar and self-service restaurant) by the car park is this smart restaurant serving Mediterranean dishes with a fixed menu. Fabulous views over the Llobregat Valley.

② RESTAURANT ABAT CISNEROS
Monestir de Montserrat; Hotel Abat Cisneros; tel: 93 877 77 01; €€€
Within the Hotel Abat Cisneros, also in the complex, is this restaurant, with a 16th-century stone dining room (the former stables) carved out of the rock. Excellent, traditional Catalan dishes are offered here, both *à la carte* and as a set menu.

deposits up to 50 million years ago, make for an unforgettable experience.

The **Via Crucis** (Way of the Cross) begins behind the Plaça de l'Abat Oliba, named after the powerful 14th-century founder of the monastery, who is celebrated in some of the many statues around the monastery. The stations of the cross were all designed by well-known artists in the early 20th century.

From Plaça de la Creu the **Funicular de la Santa Cova** runs down to the start of a 15-minute walk to Santa Cova. This chapel is in a grotto where La Moreneta is said to have been hidden in the Moorish occupation.

Highest Point

Not to be mised is the seven-minute ride on the Funicular de Sant Joan, rising at a gradient of 62 degrees high above the monastery. At the top is the **Aula de Natura** information centre and three different directions for walking, with great views down over the far side of the mountain. **Sant Jeroni**, the highest point at 1,236m (4,055ft), is a leisurely 60-minute walk away.

Above from far left: inside the basilica; cable car; the monastery's spectacular location high in the mountains; copies of La Morenata for sale.

Hunted Hermits
The caves of Montserrat were once a favoured place for hermits, but only when one died could another take his place. When Napoleon's troops arrived in the early 19th century, the hermits were 'hunted down like wild goats' and killed.

Wildlife on the Mountain

Wherever you walk on these mountains, be on the lookout for plants, butterflies, reptiles and birds that you may never have encountered before. Wild boar, red squirrel, beech marten and cat-like genet all live here, although you will be lucky to spot them, as they are adept at keeping hidden among the forests of yew, box and, most abundantly, evergreen oak. Laburnum and honeysuckle weave thickets for them, too. Rosemary and thyme scent the hills, which, in spring, are coloured with rockrose, broom and alpine flowers – in fact the Montserrat Natural Park is home to some 1,250 plant varieties. Birds to look – or listen – out for on the craggy heights include warblers, Bonelli's eagles and peregrine falcon. Down on the rocks, vipers, salamanders and lizards like to sun themselves. A good reference point for the wildlife of Montserrat is the Aula de Natura (nature centre; *see above*) at the top of the Funicular de Sant Joan.

DIRECTORY

A user-friendly alphabetical listing of practical information,
plus hand-picked hotels and restaurants, clearly organised
by area, to suit all budgets and tastes.

A

ADMISSION CHARGES

Most museums have an entry charge, with the usual reductions for children, students and the over 65s. The Articket (€20) allows entry to Barcelona's seven main museums for six months (www.articketbcn.org).

AGE RESTRICTIONS

The legal age for buying and consuming tobacco and alcohol is 18. You must be 21 to hire a car.

C

CHILDREN

Children under five go free on public transport but pay full price from five upwards. However, child fares do apply on the Tourist Bus and Tourist Cards for children aged 4–12. In museums the age at which children go free, or get in at a reduced price, varies.

Some larger hotels have childcare services. For babysitters, try Tender Loving Canguros (www.barcelonacon nect. com and www.tlcanguros.com).

CLIMATE

Barcelona's mild Mediterranean climate assures sunshine most of the year and makes freezing temperatures very rare, even during the depths of winter (December to February). Spring and autumn are the most agreeable seasons for visiting. Midsummer can be hot and humid; at times a thick mist hangs over the city. Average temperatures are 10°C (54°F) in winter, and 25°C (75°F) in summer. Rain tends to fall in November and February to March.

CLOTHING

Barcelonans are generally stylish, and dress codes are informal but elegant. Men are expected to wear jackets in the more upmarket restaurants. Jeans are fine for informal spots, but you will not see many local people eating out in shorts and trainers, except at beach-side cafés. From November to April you will need a warm jacket or sweater and raincoat. The rest of the year, light summer clothing is in order, with a hat or umbrella in case of showers.

CRIME AND SAFETY

Be on your guard against pickpockets and bag snatchers (be wary of people offering 'assistance' or becoming suddenly interested in you), especially in the Rambla and Old Town, as well as at major tourist sights. Try to avoid deserted alleyways, especially at night. Do not leave luggage unattended; do not carry more money than you need for daily expenses; use the hotel safe for larger sums and valuables; photocopy personal documents and leave the originals in your hotel; wear cameras strapped across your body; do not leave video cameras, car stereos and valuables on view in a car. The blue-clad, mobile anti-crime squads are out in force on the

Rambla and principal thoroughfares. Should you be a crime victim, make a report *(denuncia)* at the nearest police station *(comisaría)* – vital for insurance claims. The main one in the Old Town is at Nou de la Rambla, 76–78, or call the Mossos d'Esquadra (088 or 112).

CUSTOMS

As Spain is in the European Union (EU), free exchange of non-duty-free items for personal use is permitted between Spain and other EU countries (300 cigarettes, limited amounts of alcohol and perfume). Visitors may bring up to €6,000 into or out of Spain without a declaration. If you intend to bring in and take out larger sums, declare this on arrival and departure.

D

DISABLED TRAVELLERS

The city has many hotels with facilities (see www.bcn.es/turisme, or check with the tourist office). Many museums and historic buildings are wheelchair-accessible. The beaches have suitable access, and there are 14 adapted public toilets. Some bus and metro lines have facilities for disabled travellers (see www.tmb.net). For taxi information, contact 93 420 80 88.

For further information, see www.tourspain.co.uk/disabled or contact Institut Municipal de Persones amb Disminució (Avinguda Diagonal 233, 08013 Barcelona; tel: 93 413 27 75; sap@mail.bcn.es).

E

ELECTRICITY

The standard is 220 volts, but some hotels have a voltage of 110–120 in the bathrooms as a safety precaution. Check before plugging in any of your appliances.

Power sockets (outlets) take round, two-pin plugs, so British plugs do not fit and you will probably need an international adapter plug. Visitors from North America will also need a transformer, unless they have dual-voltage travel appliances.

EMBASSIES AND CONSULATES

Most Western European countries have consulates in Barcelona. All the embassies are in Madrid.

Australia: Gran Vía Carles III 98, 9º; tel: 93 330 94 96.
Canada: Carrer d'Elisenda de Pinós 10; tel: 93 204 27 00.
Ireland: Gran Vía Carles III 94; tel: 93 491 50 21.
UK: Avinguda Diagonal 477, 13º; tel. 93 366 62 00.
US: Passeig de la Reina Elisenda 23; tel: 93 280 22 27.

EMERGENCIES

General emergencies: 112
Mossos d'Esquadra (Autonomous Catalan Police): 088
Municipal (city) police: 092
Fire: 080

Above from far left: Christopher Columbus surveys the port; Mercat de Santa Caterina.

Etiquette
Barcelona is a fairly relaxed, informal city, yet it is always worth paying attention to local etiquette. It is respectful to cover up when visiting churches. Shaking hands is a common form of greeting, and physical contact, such as back patting, is a friendly gesture. Air kissing, touching right cheeks first, then the left, comes later. When addressing a stranger, the familiar *tú* is used more often than the formal *vosotros*.

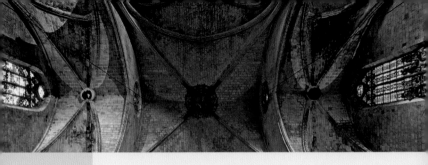

G

GAY AND LESBIAN TRAVELLERS

Barcelona has an active gay community and scores of clubs and nightlife options. Conservative Catholic beliefs still predominate in some sectors, so gay visitors may wish to be discreet. The gay and lesbian hotline is 900 601 601. The free magazine *Nois* has information and listings of clubs, restaurants and other entertainment options. Casal Lambda is a gay cultural centre (Carrer de Verdaguer i Callis 10; tel: 93 319 55 50; email: infor@ lambaweb.org; open from 5pm).

The nearby town of Sitges, just half an hour south of the city on the coast, is a real mecca for gay people, particularly in summer, and is well worth a visit *(see pp.88–91)*.

GOVERNMENT

Spain is a constitutional monarchy headed by King Juan Carlos I, who appoints the prime minister from the majority party. The parliament *(Cortes)* has a Chamber of Deputies (Lower House) with 350 members elected by proportional representation every four years. Catalonia is one of 14 autonomous regions, which elect a total of 49 members to the Senate. The autonomous region of Catalonia is governed by the Generalitat in Plaça de Sant Jaume opposite the Ajuntament (town hall), where the mayor and the city council preside.

H

HEALTH

Standards of hygiene are high, and medical care is generally excellent; most doctors speak sufficient English.

It is wise to ease yourself into the climate and food gently. In the summer, is it advisable to wear a hat and suncream when out and about during the day. You should also avoid any tired-looking tapas, particularly those that are mayonnaise-based, during the hotter months, as these could be a possible source of infection. The water is safe to drink, but can have a strong taste; bottled water is inexpensive.

EU citizens with corresponding health insurance facilities are entitled to medical and hospital treatment under the Spanish social security system – you need a **European Health Insurance Card**, obtainable from post offices or online. However, it is always advisable to take out private medical insurance, which should be part of a travel insurance package.

In an emergency, go to the *Urgencias* department of a main hospital:
Hospital de la Santa Creu i Sant Pau: Carrer de Sant Antoni Maria Claret 167; tel: 93 436 47 11 (behind the Sagrada Família).
Hospital Clinic: Carrer de Casanova 143; tel: 93 227 54 00.
Hospital Cruz Roja: Carrer del Dos de Maig 301; tel: 93 433 15 51.

For an ambulance, go to an *ambulatorio* (medical centre) or call 061 or 93 300 20 20.

Pharmacies *(farmàcia)* operate as a first line of defence, as pharmacists can prescribe drugs and are usually adept at making on-the-spot diagnoses. There is always one in each district that stays open all night and on public holidays.

HOLIDAYS

Many bars, restaurants and museums close in the afternoon and evening on public holidays and Sundays. August is the annual holiday month, and many businesses, including restaurants, may close down for three or four weeks.

1 Jan: *Año Nuevo* (New Year's Day)
6 Jan: *Epifanía* (Epiphany)
1 May: *Fiesta de Trabajo* (Labour Day)
24 June: *San Juan* (St John's Day)
15 Aug: *Asunción* (Assumption)
11 Sept: *La Diada*
(Catalan National Day)
24 Sept: *La Mercè* (Day of Mercedes, Barcelona's patron saint)
1 Nov: *Todos los Santos*
(All Saints' Day)
6 Dec: *Día de la Constitución*
(Constitution Day)
8 Dec: *Inmaculada Concepció*
(Immaculate Conception)
25–26 Dec: *Navidad* (Christmas)

Movable Feasts:
Feb/Mar: *Mardi Gras* (Shrove Tuesday/Carnival)
Late Mar/Apr: *Viernes Santo*
(Good Friday)
Late Mar/Apr: *Lunes de Pascua*
(Easter Monday)
Mid-June: *Corpus Christi*
(Corpus Christi)

INTERNET

There are numerous places where internet access is cheap and easy. Try easyInternet Café (La Rambla 31 and Ronda de la Universitat 35; both open 24 hours a day); Net-Movil (La Rambla 130; daily 10am–midnight).

L

LANGUAGE

English is understood by a large number people working in the tourist industry. Both Catalan *(català)* and Castilian Spanish *(castellano)* are official languages in Catalonia; you can assume that everyone in Barcelona who speaks Catalan can speak Spanish, but because many residents come to the city from other parts of the country, they will not all speak Catalan. Street signs are in Catalan, but labels in museums and menus are usually in both languages. Learning some Catalan will be appreciated *(see back cover of pull-out map for a few helpful phrases)*, but Spanish (Castilian) will certainly get you by.

LEFT LUGGAGE

Left-luggage lockers *(consigna)* are available in the main railway stations (Sants, Estació de França and Passeig de Gràcia) and at Barcelona Nord bus station. The left-luggage office at the sea terminal on Moll de Barcelona is open 8am–1am.

Above from far left: Santa Maria del Mar; shopping in the Eixample.

Dentists
The cost of dental care in Spain for non-Spaniards is not covered by any of the reciprocal agreements between countries, so make sure your that travel insurance covers treatment. In the case of an emergency, visit the Clínica Dental Barcelona (Passeig de Gràcia 97; tel: 93 487 83 29; emergency service daily 9am–midnight). English-speaking dentists available.

LOST PROPERTY

There is a lost property office at Carrer de la Ciutat 9, just off Plaça de Sant Jaume; 9.30am–1pm; tel: 906 427 017.

M

MEDIA

Newspapers: A large number of European newspapers and the Paris-based *International Herald Tribune* are sold on the day of publication at news-stands on La Rambla and the Passeig de Gràcia, as well as in Fnac on Plaça de Catalunya. Principal European and American magazines are also widely available in the city.

Metropolitan, Barcelona's monthly magazine in English, is free and has useful listings. For Spanish speakers, the handy *Guía del Ocio* lists bars, restaurants, and cinema, theatre and concert performances.

Television: The principal Spanish channels are TVE1 and TVE2 (state-owned), TV3 and Canal 33, the autonomous Catalan channels. The local channel is BTV. Commercial channels include Antena 3 (general programming), Tele 5 (daytime TV, directed at housewives) and Canal Plus (mainly films, for subscribers only).

Maps
These are freely distributed by the tourist offices, and often left out for tourists in hotel rooms. There are also useful local wall maps at all metro stations.

MONEY

Currency: The monetary unit of Spain is the euro (abbreviate to €). Notes are issued in denominations of 5, 10, 20, 50, 100, 200 and 500 euros. Coins in circulation are 1, 2, 5, 10, 20 and 50 centimos and 1 and 2 euros.

Currency Exchange: Banks and *cajas/caixes* (savings banks) are usually the best places to exchange currency, as they offer the most competitive rates with no commission. *Casas de cambio* (displaying a *cambio* sign) are convenient in that they open outside banking hours. Those advertising 'no commission' have lower exchange rates so you will in effect pay a hefty commission. Banks and exchange offices pay slightly more for travellers' cheques than for cash. Always take your passport when you go to change money.

Credit Cards: These are widely recognised, though smaller businesses tend to prefer cash. Photo identification is usually requested when paying with a card.

Cash Machines: These are ubiquitous. With displays in several languages, they will dispense money against your debit or credit card in just the same way that they do at home, using the same PIN.

Travellers' Cheques: Hotels, shops, restaurants and travel agencies all cash travellers' cheques, but banks generally give a better rate – you will always need your passport. Cash small amounts at a time, and keep the individual numbers of your cheques separately so they can be replaced quickly if they are lost or stolen.

O

OPENING TIMES

Banks: These generally open Mon–Fri 8.30am–2pm, and also Sat 9am–1pm in winter.

Businesses: These open Mon–Fri 9am–2pm and 4–8pm. In summer, many office workers do *horas intensivas* (intensive hours) from 8am–3pm, to enable them to go home before the hottest part of the day.

Museums: Most are open Tue–Sat 9am–1pm and 4–8pm, and Sun 10am–2.30pm. The majority close on Mon, but there are exceptions.

Restaurants: Many close on Sun, and some close on Mon.

Shops: The big department stores remain open throughout the day, from 10am–9.30pm, while most other shops close for lunch in the early afternoon. Usual hours are Mon–Sat 9am–1.30pm and 4–8pm.

P

POLICE

The municipal and autonomous Catalan police are efficient and courteous – and generally very responsive to issues involving foreign tourists. In Barcelona, dial 092 for municipal (city) police and 088 for the autonomous Catalan police. The main police station in the Old Town is at Nou de la Rambla 76–8.

POST

The Central Post Office *(correus)* is in Plaça d'Antoni López, at the bottom of Via Laietana, in the vicinity of the port area (tel: 93 216 04 53; Mon–Fri 9am–9pm, Sat 9am–1pm).

Stamps can be purchased at the post office or at a tobacconists – look for the brown-and-yellow sign that reads '*Tabacs*'. Rates are divided into four areas of the world, just like telephone calls: the EU, rest of Europe, the US and Canada, and the rest of the world. Allow about one week for delivery to North America, and 4–5 days to the UK. To speed things up, send a letter *urgente* (express) or *certificado* (registered).

R

RELIGION

Roman Catholicism is the religion of Catalonia (and all Spain) and Mass is said regularly in the churches of Barcelona. There are churches of most major faiths; the tourist information at Plaça de Catalunya has details on religious services, and those in foreign languages. Major ones include:
Anglican: St George's Church; Carrer de Sant Joan de la Salle 41; tel: 93 417 88 67; Sun 11am.
Judaism: Synagogue: Carrer de l'Avenir 24; tel: 93 200 61 48.
Islam: Centro Islàmico; Avinguda Meridiana 326; tel: 93 351 49 01.

Above from far left: nuns in El Born; there are numerous ways to spend your money in Barcelona.

S

SPORT

Bicycles: Cycle lanes in the centre are well marked, and the traffic-free port, marinas and beach front are also great for cycling. Bikes can be rented at several outlets, such as Icària Sports (Avinguda d' Icària 180; tel: 93 221 17 78) and from Filicletos (Passeig de Picasso 40; tel: 93 319 78 11), from where there is easy access to the Parc de la Ciutadella and the waterfront (tandems and child seats available). Barcelona by Bicycle (tel: 93 268 21 05) offers tours around El Born, Sant Pere, the Gothic Quarter, and the waterfront – one even includes dinner. They also hire bikes. Contact Amics de la Bici (Carrer de Demóstenes 19; tel/fax: 93 339 40 60) for more information.

Golf: There are many golf courses all over Catalonia: for a full list, see www.gencat.net/probert. Weekend fees are usually double the weekday fee. Three courses close to Barcelona are: El Prat de Llobregat (tel: 93 379 02 78), Sant Cugat (tel: 93 674 39 08) and Sitges (tel: 93 894 05 80).

Tennis: ClubVall Parc (tel: 93 212 67 89; 8am–midnight). Quite expensive.

Water Sports: Base Nautica de la Mar Bella (tel: 93 221 04 32) has all types of boats for hire by qualified sailors; sailing courses and windsurf hire too.

Spectator Sports: Check the daily papers, weekly entertainment guides or magazines such as *El Mundo Deportivo*.

T

TELEPHONES

Phone Numbers: Spain's country code is 34. Barcelona's local area code, 93, must be dialled before all phone numbers, even for local calls.

Public Phones: You can make direct-dial local, national and international calls from public phone booths in the street. Most operate with coins and cards; international phone credit cards can also be used. Instructions for use are given in several languages in the booths.

You can also make calls at public telephone offices called *locutorios*. These are much quieter than making a call on the street. The main post office has phone booths.

International Calls: Dial 00 for an international line + the country code + phone number, omitting any initial zero. The country code for the UK is 44, for the US and Canada it is 1, and for Australia, 61. Calls are cheaper after 10pm on weekdays, after 2pm on Saturday, and all day Sunday.

For general telephone information, dial 1003. For international calls, dial 1005, for national calls, 1009.

TIME DIFFERENCES

Spanish time is the same as that in most of Western Europe – Greenwich

Smoking
Lighting up is banned in all public places, including on public transport, in offices, shops, schools, hospitals and theatres. Restaurants larger than 102 sq m (1,100 sq ft) must have smoking sections. Smaller restaurants and bars have, for the moment, the choice of being smoking or non-smoking establishments.

Mean Time plus one hour. Daylight Savings Time is in effect from the last Sunday in March to the last Sunday in September; clocks go forward one hour in spring and back one hour in autumn, so Spain is generally one hour ahead of London, the same as Paris, and six hours ahead of New York.

TIPPING

There are no golden rules. If you feel the need to leave a tip, make it a token rather than an extravagant one. Some restaurants automatically add a service charge to the total, in which case nothing extra is needed. As a yardstick, in restaurants where a charge is not added, it should be around 5–10 percent and about the same in a taxi. In a bar or café, 80 centimos–€1.50 is enough, depending on the size of the bill.

TOURIST INFORMATION

For general information call the Barcelona Tourist Office (tel: 010), or contact Turespaña (tel: 900 300 600). The main tourist office is Turisme de Barcelona (Plaça de Catalunya 17; tel: 906 301 282; if calling from abroad, tel: 93 368 97 30; hotel information tel: 93 304 32 32; open daily 9am–9pm).

The Tourism Information Office in the Ajuntament (Town Hall), Plaça de Sant Jaume, is open Mon–Sat 8am– 8pm, Sun and public hols 8am– 2pm.

Informació Turística de Catalunya (Palau Robert, Passeig de Gràcia 107; tel: 93 238 40 00; Mon–Fri 10am– 7pm, Sat 10am–2pm; www.gen cat.es/probert) provides information about the whole region.

There are also information offices at Sants station (Mon–Sat 8am–10pm), and the airport (Arrivals Hall; tel: 93 478 47 04; Mon–Sat 9.30am–8pm, Sun 9.30am–3pm).

Australia: International House, Suite 44, 104 Bathurst Street, P.O. Box A-675, 2000 Sydney NSW; tel: 02 264 79 66.

Canada: 2 Bloor Street West, Suite 3402, Toronto, Ontario, M4W 3E2; tel: 416 961 3131.

UK: 79 New Cavendish Street, London, W1W 6XB; tel: 020 7486 8077; brochure line; tel: 09063 640 630. Note that this office is open to the public by appointment only.

US: Water Tower Place, Suite 915 East, 845 North Michigan Avenue, Chicago, IL 60611; tel: 312 944 0216/642 1992.

8383 Wilshire Boulevard, Suite 960, 90211 Beverly Hills, CA 90211; tel: 213 658 7188.

666 5th Avenue, 35th floor, New York, NY 10103; tel: 212 265 8822.

1221 Brickell Avenue, Miami, FL 33131; tel: 305 358 1992.

TOURS

Guides: Licensed English-speaking guides and interpreters may be arranged through the Barcelona Guide Bureau (tel: 93 268 24 22; email: bgb@bcn.servicom.es) or City Guides (tel: 93 412 06 74). Hotels and travel agencies will also recommend and advise on guides.

Above from far left: advertising basketball; information centre on the Rambla.

Toilets

There are many expressions for toilets: *el serveis* or *lavabos* in Catalan; *aseos, servicios* and *WC* (say 'doobl'-vay') in Castilian. Toilet doors are distinguished by a 'C' for *Caballeros* (gentlemen) or 'S' for *Señoras* (ladies) or by a variety of pictographs.
In addition to the well-marked public toilets in main squares and stations, a number of neat coin-operated toilets in portable cabins marked 'WC' are installed around the city. Just about every bar and restaurant has a toilet available for public use. It is considered polite to buy a drink if you drop in to use the conveniences.

Bus Tours: The Barcelona Bus Turístic offers a tour of 24 city sights with two different routes, and you can get on and off as you please. Both routes depart from Plaça de Catalunya at 9am daily, and there are full timetables at all stops. The complete journey time is about 3 hours. Buy tickets on-board or in advance at Turisme de Barcelona (Plaça de Catalunya; tel: 906 301 282).

An air-conditioned bus, rather unfortunately called the 'Tomb Bus', runs during business hours from the Plaça de Catalunya to the uptown Plaça Maria Cristina, covering all the up-market shopping areas.

On Foot: Barcelona Walking Tours has English-speaking guided tours of the Barri Gòtic every Saturday and Sunday at 10am. Walks (lasting about 90 minutes) begin at Turisme de Barcelona (Plaça de Catalunya; tel: 906 301 282). At 10.30am on Saturdays and Sundays there is also a Picasso tour. Walks should be booked in advance at a tourist office.

By Bicycle: Barcelona by Bicycle (Carrer d'Espartería 3; tel: 93 268 21 05) leads easy-going bike tours around the Old Town and the waterfront (one tour also includes dinner). The Montjuïc 'mcard', which gives reduced prices for museum entry, also includes bike hire.

Out of Town: Popular tours include visits to Montserrat, Sitges, the Penedès wine region and Dalí country – useful if you do not wish to drive in the region.

TRANSPORT

Arrival

By Air: Barcelona's airport is linked by regularly scheduled daily non-stop flights from across Europe. Some flights from the US, Canada and New Zealand are direct; others go through Madrid. Flying time from London is about 2 hours; from New York, it takes about 8 hours.

Iberia, the Spanish national airline, covers most countries in shared arrangements with their national carriers (Iberia House, 10 Hammersmith Broadway, London W6 7AL; tel: 08456 012 854; www.iberia.com). They are a member of Opodo (www.opodo.co.uk), the internet online booking service that gives the cheapest deals among a number of carriers. Good charter airline deals can be found.

The international airport, El Prat de Llobregat (tel: 93 298 38 38), is 12km (7 miles) south of the city centre and has three terminals. There are tourist information and hotel reservation booths in Terminal B.

The city can be reached by train or by bus. The national train service, Renfe, runs trains from opposite the airport every half hour, stopping at Estació de Sants, Plaça de Catalunya and Estació de França, taking 20–30 minutes. The fare is about €3. The Aerobús departs every 12 minutes from all three terminals for Sants and Plaça de Catalunya (Mon–Sat 6am–11pm, Sun 6.30am–10.45pm; for €4 single, €6 return).

Taxis charge about €20 to the city centre. Agree a fare before you start.

By Sea: Barcelona has good sea links to the Balearic Islands and Genoa in Italy. Buquebus (tel: 971 40 09 69; fax: 971 29 10 09; www.buquebus.com) is the fastest Mallorca ferry (3 hours). Trasmediterránea (Moll Sant Bertran 3; tel: 93 295 91 00; www.trasmediterranea.es) also operates ferries to the Balearic islands; most of the year they take 8 hours and in summer there is an express ferry that takes about 4 hours.

By Rail: Passengers have to change trains at the Spanish frontier, as the Spanish tracks are of a wider gauge than the French. Exceptions are the luxury high-speed TALGO and the Trans-Europ-Express, which have adjustable axles. The TALGO arrives at Estació de França.

Renfe, the Spanish national rail network (tel: 90 224 34 02 for international trains; www.renfe.es), honours Inter-Rail, Rail-Europ and Eurail cards (the latter sold only outside Europe), and offers substantial discounts for people aged under 26 and over 65.

By Car: The AP7 motorway leads to Barcelona from France 160km (100 miles) to the north. The AP2 leads to Barcelona from Madrid, Zaragoza and Bilbao. From Valencia or the Costa del Sol, take the E-15 north. Your car should display a nationality sticker.

Within Barcelona

Barcelona has a reliable and comprehensive public transport system; getting around town is easy, rapid and inexpensive. Get an up-to-date bus and train *(feve)* timetable from a tourist information office or any metro station. Information on all public transport: tel: 010; Mon–Sat 8am–10pm; www.tmb.net. An integrated system means that tickets can be used on buses, trams or trains: best to buy a book of 10 (the *T-10*), which works out about the same as buying six single tickets.

By Bus: Routes and timetables are clearly marked, and maps are available from the tourist office. If it is your first time in the city, you may have trouble recognising where you are, and most bus drivers speak no English. With the metro, it is easier to identify your stop. But buses are a good way of getting to see more of the city. They run daily 6am–11pm; there are infrequent night buses from 10.30pm–5am.

By Metro: Modern, clean and efficient, the metro is by far the fastest and easiest way to navigate the city. The metro runs Mon–Thur 5am–11pm, Fri and Sat 5am–2am; holidays 6am–11pm and Sun 6am–midnight. Good pocket-sized maps are available at metro stations.

By Train: Regional FGC (Ferrocarrils Generalitat de Catalunya) trains also travel to Barcelona's upper neighbourhoods Gràcia, Sarrià, Pedralbes and Tibidabo and to nearby towns such as Terrassa and Sabadell. Unless you are going to one of these destinations, make sure the train you board (most likely at Plaça de Catalunya) is a metro

Above from far left: on board a Golondrina touring boat; cable car from Montjuïc.

and not an FGC train – it is easy to confuse them.

By Taxi: Black-and-yellow taxis are everywhere and not too expensive. During the day, they are not your best option, as traffic is heavy. At night, especially if you have dined in the Old Town, taxis are the best way to return to your hotel or continue on with the night (have the restaurant call one if you do not feel comfortable waiting on the street). Hail a cab in the street or pick one up where they are lined up (usually outside hotels). A green light and/or a *libre* (vacant) sign shows when the cab is empty.

Reputable taxi companies include Radio Móvil (tel: 93 358 11 11), Radiotaxi Verd (tel: 93 266 39 39) and Taxigroc (tel: 93 490 22 22). Check the fare before you get in; rates are fixed and are displayed in several languages on the window. Also ensure that the meter has been reset when you begin your journey. Refuse a cab if the driver claims the meter is not working.

Driving

Car Hire (Rental): Unless you plan to travel a good deal throughout Catalonia, there is no need to rent a car.

Major international companies and Spanish companies have offices in the airport and in the city centre. A value-added tax (IVA) of 15 percent is added to the total charge, but will have been included if you have pre-paid before

Right: the cathedral soars over the Barri Gòtic.

arrival (normally the way to obtain the lowest rates). Fully comprehensive insurance is required and should be included in the price; confirm that this is the case. Most companies require you to pay by credit card, or use your card as a deposit/guarantee. You must be over 21 and have had a licence for at least 6 months. A national driver's licence will suffice for EU nationals; others need an international licence.

Drivers must be able, at any time, to produce a passport, a valid driver's licence, registration papers and Green Card international insurance, which comes with a Bail Bond from your insurance company.

Rules and Regulations: Front and rear seatbelts are compulsory. Most fines for traffic offences are payable on the spot. Driving rules are the same as those that apply throughout continental Europe: drive on the right, overtake on the left, give right of way to vehicles coming from the right (unless your road is marked as having priority). Do not drink and drive. The permitted blood-alcohol level is low and penalties stiff.

Speed Limits: These are: 120kph (75 mph) on motorways, 100kph (62 mph) on dual carriageways, 90kph (56mph) on main roads, and 50kph (30 mph), or as marked, in urban areas.

Emergencies: In the case of a breakdown or other emergency, tel: 112. On motorways there are SOS boxes.

Parking: Finding a place to park can be extremely difficult. Look for 'blue zones' (denoted by a blue 'P'), which are metered areas; or underground parking garages (also marked with a big blue-and-white 'P'). Green zones are reserved for residents with permits.

VISAS AND PASSPORTS

Visas are needed by non-EU nationals unless their country has a reciprocal agreement with Spain. Full information on passport and visa regulations is available from the Spanish Embassy.

W

WEBSITES

These websites offer useful information about Barcelona and its surroundings:
• Barcelona Ajuntament (City Hall): www.bcn.es
• Barcelona on the web: www.aboutbarcelona.com
• Barcelona Tourist Information: www.barcelonaturisme.com
• Catalonia on the web: www.gencat.es
• Spain on the web: www.spaintour.com
• National Tourist Office: www.tourspain.es
• Transport information: www.tmb.net

WEIGHTS AND MEASURES

In common with most of Europe, Spain uses the metric system.

Above from far left: the atmospheric Old Town; taking a break on La Rambla.

Weight/Distance Conversions
To convert kilometres into miles divide by 1.6093; to convert metres into feet divide by 0.3048; to convert kilogrammes into pounds divide by 0.4536; to convert hectares into acres divide by 0.4047. To convert from imperial to metric multiply by the factor shown. If this all sounds too complicated, it is simpler to bear in mind that a kilometre is roughly five-eighths of a mile; a metre is roughly three feet/one yard; a kilogramme is just over 2lb, a litre is just under two pints, or a fifth of a gallon, and a hectare is about two-and-a-half acres.

La Rambla

1898

La Rambla 109; tel: 93 552 95 52; www.nnhotels.com; €€€€

The year of 1898 was when the Philippines gained independence from Spain, and the building was until then the headquarters of the Philippines Tobacco company. Now it is a swish hotel, right on the Rambla, with sound-proofed rooms and an up-market colonial elegance that makes you want to puff on a pipe and talk about conditions on the estates.

Citadines Barcelona-Ramblas

La Rambla 122; tel: 93 270 11 11; www.citadines.com; €€€

An excellent-value apartment-hotel with a pleasant breakfast buffet bar and good views from the rooftop. Food shopping can be done at the nearby Boquería market *(see p.31)*.

Continental

La Rambla 138; tel: 93 301 25 70; www.hotelcontinental.com; €€

In a prime position near the top of La Rambla, this is an historic hotel with individual character. Swirling carpets and floral décor can be forgiven when you can sit on a balcony watching the world go by – at a reasonable price. Ask for a room at the front.

Ginebra

Rambla de Catalunya 1; tel: 93 317 1063; €€

This place is on the simple, basic side – not all rooms have en-suite bathrooms, for example. However, it is extremely clean, the staff are friendly, and the location is central, with views of Plaça de Catalunya from some rooms. All windows are double-glazed, which helps in this busy part of the city. Good value for money.

Kabul

Plaça Reial 17; tel: 93 318 51 90; www.kabul.es; €

Long-established youth hostel in a privileged position on this grand square just off La Rambla. Rooms extend to dormitories for up to 20 guests. Known for its party atmosphere.

Oriente

La Rambla 45; tel: 93 302 25 58; www.husa.es; €€€

Once a charismatic old favourite, after refurbishment it has recovered some of its former glory, including the splendid ballroom, but at the expense of some of its personality.

Barri Gòtic

Catalonia Albinoni

Avinguda del Portal de l'Àngel 17; tel: 93 318 41 41; www.hoteles-catalonia.es; €€€

A relatively new hotel housed in a stylish old building on one of Bar-

Price guide for a double room for one night with breakfast:	
€€€€	over 200 euros
€€€	140–200 euros
€€	70–140 euros
€	below 70 euros

celona's busiest pedestrian shopping streets. Rooms are large and well-furnished, and there is a very nice garden patio. A good choice if you want to be in the thick of things.

Gran Hotel Barcino

Carrer de Jaume I 6; tel: 93 302 20 12; www.hotelbarcino.com; €€€

In the heart of the Barri Gòtic, this modern hotel is chic and very well designed. The large, airy lobby does, however, outclass the rooms.

Call

Carrer de l'Arc de Sant Ramon del Call 4; tel: 93 302 11 23; €

A clean, small, air-conditioned 1-star hotel in the shady lanes of the Barri Gòtic. No bar or restaurant but everything you want is on your doorstep.

Gotico

Carrer de Jaume I 14; tel: 93 315 22 11; www.hotelgotico.com; €€€

In one of the Barri Gòtic's main streets, this sound-proofed hotel has 81 rooms, some with terrace, and a sundeck. Thoroughly modern, and though in the best possible taste, it is handy, light and clean.

Jardí

Plaça de Sant Josep Oriol 1; tel: 93 301 59 00; €€

Small hotel in the Barri Gòtic, overlooking two of the prettiest plazas in Barcelona. The rooms are a bargain, although a plaza view costs a little more. Recently renovated and very popular so book well ahead.

Levante

Baixada de Sant Miquel 7; tel: 93 317 95 65; www.hostallevante.com; €

Basic accommodation with friendly atmosphere (and price). Prides itself on the tale that the young Picasso was a frequent visitor in its former life as a house of ill repute. Situated just off Carrer d'Avinyó, one of the trendiest streets in the area.

Neri

Carrer de Sant Sever 5; tel: 93 304 06 55; www.hotelneri.com; €€€

Elegant boutique hotel in a 17th-century palace overlooking one of the Gothic quarter's most atmospheric squares near the cathedral. The roof terrace has views over medieval spires. Only 22 rooms.

Nouvel Hotel

Carrer de Santa Ana 18–20; tel: 93 301 82 74; www.hotelnouvel.com; €€€

On a pedestrianised street between La Rambla and Portal d'Àngel, in an atmospheric area, this small hotel has a wonderful Modernista lobby and dining room. Rooms are plainer, but spacious and well equipped.

Racó del Pi

Carrer Pi 7; tel: 93 342 6190; www.h10.es; €€€

Set in the very heart of the Barri Gòtic, around the corner from the Plaça del Pi, this small hotel has been built within an old palace. There are only 37 rooms so it tends to get booked up early.

Above from far left: flowers in reception; Casa Camper *(see p.116).*

Self-catering
Tourist-let flats are becoming ever more popular, especially with families, as they offer the opportunity to self-cater, enabling shopping in the market and cutting holiday costs. Browse websites www.flatsby days.com or www. oh-barcelona.com, which have a range of flats on their books. For a more luxurious option, try www.cru2001.com.

Fortunately for the Northern European and North American tourists who take their holidays in mid-summer, July and August are not considered peak times in hotel terms; September and October are in fact the peak months, when rooms will be more expensive and harder to find.

Sant Pere, La Ribera and El Born

Banys Orientals

Carrer de l'Argenteria 37; tel: 93 268 84 60; www.hotelbanysorientals.com; €€

One of the best options in town, with impeccable slick interiors and stylish details, and it is in the hottest spot for shopping, wining and dining. On the ground floor is the excellent restaurant Senyor Parellada *(see p.121)*. Unbeatable value, so book well in advance.

Chic&basic

Carrer de la Princesa 50; tel: 93 295 46 52; www.chicandbasic.com; €€

Latest on the scene, this stylish, ultramodern hotel is situated in a handsome 19th-century building, well located between the Parc de la Ciutadella and the trendy El Born area. Surprisingly good value.

Park Hotel

Avinguda del Marquès de l'Argentera 11; tel: 93 319 60 00; www.park hotelbarcelona.com; €€€

A gem of 1950s architecture, quite rare in Barcelona, opposite the Estació de França, and near the Parc de la Ciutadella. It is on the edge of the Born

Price guide for a double room for one night with breakfast:

€€€€	over 200 euros
€€€	140–200 euros
€€	70–140 euros
€	below 70 euros

district, which is awash with cafés, restaurants and bars and within walking distance of the Barceloneta beach. The rooms are well designed in neutral colours.

Pensió 2000

Carrer Sant Pere Més Alt 6, 1st floor; tel: 93 310 7466; €€

An elegant marble staircase leads to this friendly family-run guesthouse, which is a cut above the average *pension* and right opposite the Palau de la Música Catalana. Great value.

Pension Ciudadela

Carrer del Comercio, 33, 1st floor; tel: 93 319 62 03; €

Opposite the Estació de França, this humble guesthouse has decent rooms at a very reasonable price, and is within staggering distance of the Born nightlife.

El Raval

Casa Camper

Carrer d'Elisabets 11; tel: 93 342 62 80; www.casacamper.com; €€€

The first hotel to be opened by the sunny Mallorcan shoemakers is as chic as you might expect; 25 rooms designed by Fernando Amat of Vinçon and Jordi Tió in an imposing 19th-century building.

España

Carrer de Sant Pau 11; tel: 93 318 17 58; www.hotelespanya.com; €€–€€€

Just off the lower part of La Rambla, the España retains enough flavour of

bygone days to recommend it. The beautiful public rooms were all designed by the Modernista architect Domènech i Montaner. Guest rooms are plain but clean and large. No air conditioning.

Gat Raval

Carrer de Joaquin Costa 42, 2nd floor; tel: 93 481 66 70; www.gataccommodation.com; €€

Bright, colourful and designed to attract the young, aware traveller, this is a basic but fun hostal overlooking the MACBA *(see p.51)*. Only eight of the 24 rooms are en suite, and there is no bar or restaurant kitchen. Its sister hostal, Hostal Gat Xino, is also situated in the Raval. irresi

Grau

Carrer Ramelleres 27; tel: 93 301 8135; €€

Book early for this popular, well-kept pension, which is in a good position for shopping and visiting both the Eixample and Old Town alike. Excellent breakfasts in the adjoining bar.

Inglaterra

Carrer de Pelai 14; tel: 93 505 1100; €€–€€€

A handsome hotel set behind an old façade, and equally well located for the bohemian Raval or the elegant Eixample. Stands out from the crowd in its price range.

Peninsular

Carrer de Sant Pau 34; tel: 93 302 31 38; €€

In an old Augustian monastery, with rooms around an inner courtyard. Rooms are basic but good value for money, and staff are helpful and friendly.

The Waterfront

Arts

Passeig de la Marina 19–21; tel: 93 221 10 00: www.harts.es; €€€€

A high-tech, ultra-deluxe high-rise, situated right by the beach in Vila Olímpica. Extremely efficient, decorated with sophisticated, understated taste. Large rooms, huge bathrooms and amazing views.

Barcelona Princess

Avinguda Diagonal 1; tel: 93 356 10 00; www.princess-hotels.com; €€€€

On the cutting edge in all senses: designed by leading Catalan architect Oscar Tusquets, situated in this brand-new district of Barcelona, the Diagonal Mar, and offering all possible facilities. Prices are subject to radical cuts, too, so it is worth trying to bargain for the benefit of sleeping at this giddy height, with great views of sea and city.

Duquesa de Cardona

Passeig de Colom 12; tel: 93 268 90 90; www.hduqesadecardona.com; €€€

A classically elegant hotel set in the long-overlooked, handsome buildings giving on to the original waterfront and the old harbour. The pool and terrace on the roof are a hidden treasure. Luxury at a moderate price.

Above from far left: the view over the port, towards the Hotel Arts; in the café at the Hotel Arts.

Sea Views

There are several new hotels along the recently developed waterfront near Diagonal Mar where high standard accommodation can be found at a reasonable price. As they are a taxi or metro ride from the centre, they are less popular, but the advantage of sea views and more peaceful nights is well worth considering.

Front Marítim

Passeig de García Faria 69–71; tel: 93 303 44 40; www.hotelfront maritim.com; €€€

One of the hotels on the waterfront between the Vila Olímpica and Diagonal Mar. It is just a taxi ride away from the inner city buzz, but you wake up to sea views. Slick and comfortable.

Sea Point Hostel

Plaça del Mar 4; tel: 93 224 70 75; www.seapointhostel.com; €

An unbeatable position for a youth hostel right on Barceloneta beach. This forward-thinking chain of youth hostels also has a branch in La Ribera (Gothic Point) and one up in Gràcia (La Ciutat).

The Eixample

Actual

Carrer del Rosselló 238; tel: 93 552 05 50; www.hotelactual.com; €€€

Situated on the same block as Gaudí's La Pedrera, this well-equipped, contemporary hotel offers minimalist decor in dark brown and white combined with a warm, personal atmosphere. It is sought after, so try and book early.

Axel

Carrer d'Aribau 33; tel: 93 323 93 93; www.axelhotels.com; €€€

Voted the world's top gay boutique hotel, the chic Axel has a Modernista exterior, rooftop pool, sundeck and steam bath, and hosts regular drag shows, tea dances and high tea. Not exclusively gay, however: it claims to be 'hetero-friendly'.

Balmes Hotel

Carrer de Mallorca 216; tel: 93 451 19 14; www.derbyhotels.es; €€€

Part of the Derby Hotels chain, the Balmes promises 'the advantages of the countryside in the heart of the city', and has an attractive leafy garden and a pool. Good location.

Casa Fuster

Passeig de Gràcia 132; tel: 93 255 30 00; www.hotelescenter.es; €€€€

Classified as a five-star 'Monument' hotel, Casa Fuster, built by Domènech i Montaner in 1908, has been restored to all its Modernista splendour. Facilities include the Café Viennese, the Galaxó restaurant, a jacuzzi and gym, plus a terrace-top pool, from where there are gorgeous views of the city. A member of the Leading Small Hotels of the World.

Condes de Barcelona

Passeig de Gràcia 75; tel: 93 488 2200; www.condesdebarcelona. com; €€€

Contemporary elegance in two Modernista buildings facing each other in the Quadrat d'Or area of the Eixample. Some rooms have private balconies, and there is a roof terrace with a mini pool.

Price guide for a double room for one night with breakfast:	
€€€€	over 200 euros
€€€	140–200 euros
€€	70–140 euros
€	below 70 euros

Constanza

Carrer del Bruc 33; tel: 93 270 19 10; www.hotelconstanza.com; €€

Modern, efficient boutique hotel that should appeal to those with a funky young outlook. The rooms are not huge, but some have terraces.

Gran Hotel Havana Silken

Gran Vía de les Corts Catalanes 647; tel: 93 412 11 15; www.hotelessilken.com; €€€€

A hip and high-tech hotel in an 1872 mansion situated on Gran Via. Deluxe accommodation at a not unreasonable price. Barcelona's signature design elements are in every detail.

Girona

Carrer de Girona 24, 1st floor; tel: 93 265 02 59; www.hostalgirona.com; €

A grand stone staircase rises from the elegant patio of this Modernista building designed by Idelfons Cerdà and situated in the area known as the Quadrat d'Or. The hostal is a good-value option in a very central location, with warm, friendly reception from the Berlanga family.

Omm

Carrer del Rosselló 265; tel: 93 445 40 00; www.hotelomm.es; €€€€

Just off Passeig de Gràcia, this award-winning designer hotel is part of the seriously cool Tragaluz group. The rooms are stylish and well lit, the rooftop pool is stunning, with views of Gaudí's La Pedrera, and the in-house club is the latest place to be on Barcelona's night scene.

Paseo de Gràcia

Passeig de Gràcia 102; tel: 93 215 58 24; €€

Another vestige from the past, with some original fittings. Prime location and good value for money in this expensive area.

Prestige

Passeig de Gràcia 62; tel: 93 272 41 80; www.prestigepaseodegracia.com; €€€€

Low-key elegance in the heart of Passeig de Gràcia in this stylish newcomer. Their claim to individuality is the 'Ask Me' service: a team of switched-on young people who can answer your cultural, gastronomic or shopping queries. Experience the typical Eixample inner patio in their small, Oriental-style garden.

San Medín

Carrer Gran de Gràcia 125; tel: 93 217 30 68; www.sanmedin.com; €

There are not too many budget hotels in the upmarket Eixample, so this comfortable little pension located at the top of Passeig de Gràcia is worth knowing about.

The 5 Rooms

Carrer de Pau Claris 72, 1st floor; tel: 93 342 78 80; www.thefiverooms.com; €€

Five guest rooms make up this romantic bed-and-breakfast place, tucked away in the heart of the Eixample neighbourhood. Stylish, modern and thoughtfully decorated, it bills itself as a 'cocooning' concept to make you feel at home.

Above from far left: funky neon; hotel upkeep.

La Rambla

Amaya
La Rambla 20–4; tel: 93 302 61 38; daily L and D; €€€

Well-established Basque restaurant with a bustling bar that does snacks and an elegant dining room at the rear, where fish is the best option.

Egipte
La Rambla 79; tel: 93 317 95 45; daily L and D; €

A lively, popular place just near the Boqueria. Once a small eatery within the market itself, Egipte is now spread over several floridly decorated floors.

Fresc Co
Carrer del Carme 16; tel: 93 301 68 31; daily L and D; €

Just past the church of Betlem, this is one in a chain of self-service restaurants offering all you can eat for under €10.

Barri Gòtic

Agut
Carrer d'en Gignàs 16; tel: 93 315 17 09; Tue–Sat L and D, Sun L only; €–€€

This historic restaurant is hidden away on a small street in the Barri Gòtic.

Price guide for a three-course à-la-carte dinner for one with half a bottle of house wine:

€€€€	over 60 euros
€€€	30–60 euros
€€	20–30 euros
€	below 20 euros

Relaxed and homely, it has plenty of Catalan flavour and lots of daily specials. The excellent huge rice dishes are meant to be shared.

Agut d'Avignon
Carrer de la Trinitá; tel: 93 302 60 34; daily L and D, closed Aug; €€€€

No relation to the Agut *(above)*, this rustic restaurant is spread over several floors in an alley near the Plaça del Rei. Creative and hearty Catalan cooking and a tremendous wine cellar.

Can Culleretes
Carrer d'en Quintana 5; tel: 93 317 30 22; Tue–Sat L and D, Sun L only, closed July and Christmas; €–€€

Barcelona's oldest restaurant has served traditional Catalan food since 1786. It is cosy and informal, and has tasty classics including *espinacas à la catalana* (spinach with pine nuts and raisins) and *butifarra* (white sausage).

Los Caracoles
Carrer d'Escudellers 14; tel: 93 302 31 85; daily L and D; €€–€€€

'The Snails' is famous for its chicken on spits outside. It has been around since 1835, and, while it is touristy, it is also fun, and you can get a fine meal of fish, game, roasted chicken or lamb, in addition to the speciality *caracoles*.

Freud B'Art
Baixada de Sant Miquel, 4; tel: 93 318 66 29; Mon–Sat D only; €€–€€€

Gianni Fusco's inspired dishes are served in the laid-back atmosphere of this stylish gallery-cum-restaurant.

MEJILLONES
MORCILLAS
PATATAS BRAVAS
PATATAS ALL I OLI
PATATAS BOMBA
PISTO
PINCHO MORUNO
TORTILL...

Cal Pep
Plaça de les Olles 8; tel: 93 310 79 61; Tue–Sat L and D, Mon D only; €€€
A boisterous bar in El Born that does some of the best seafood in Barcelona. Join the cava-sipping queue for a seat at the counter where you can enjoy watching delectable little dishes being prepared for you by the spirited staff.

Espai Sucre
Carrer de la Princesa 53; tel: 93 268 16 30; Tue–Sat D only; €€€
Desserts only are served at this inventive restaurant. However, they include 'salads', 'soups' and other concoctions never found in a cake shop – or anywhere else. Excellent dessert wines accompany the 3- to 5-course meals.

Hofman
Carrer de l'Argenteria 74–8; tel: 93 319 58 89; Mon–Fri L and D; €€€€
Seriously good food cooked by Cordon Bleu chefs under the eye of Mey Hofman, who runs a cooking school here. Pricey but worth it.

Mirador
Palau de la Música Catalana, Carrer de Sant Pere Més Alt; tel: 93 310 24 33; daily L and D; €€€€
An elegant option with fine views of the Modernista concert hall. Under the watchful eye of Michelin-star chef Jean-Luc Figueras, the immaculate dishes are Catalan with French influences. Open after concerts.

Senyor Parellada
Carrer de l'Argentería 37; tel: 93 310 50 94; daily L and D; €€–€€€
An attractive, popular spot owned and run by the family that owns the adjoining Banys Orientals hotel and nearby El Vinyo del Senyor wine bar. The creative Catalan menu is sophisticated but unpretentious.

Set Portes
Passeig d'Isabel II; tel: 93 319 30 33; daily L and D; €€
Sympathetically restored, recapturing the original atmosphere, this 160-year old classic specialises in rice dishes, one for each day of the week.

Can Maxim
Carrer del Bonsuccés 8; tel: 93 302 02 34; €
Just off La Rambla, this restaurant serves a good-value, hearty set menu to local office workers. A far cry from the tourist traps on the main Rambla.

Casa Leopoldo
Carrer de Sant Rafael 24; tel: 93 441 30 14; Tue–Sat L and D, Sun D only; €€€
Tucked away in the Barri Xino, this restaurant serves excellent fish to those in the know.

Elisabets
Carrer d'Elisabets 2; tel: 93 317 58 26; Mon–Sat L, Fri D only; €
Bustling local bar that does great winter stews and a good-value set menu.

Above from far left: La Tinaja bodega in El Born (Carrer de l'Espartería 9); chocolate bars by Brunells; lunch menu; smart dining at seafood restaurant Carballeira (Carrer de la Reina Cristina 3).

Menú del Día
Lunch can be the most economical meal of the day, with nearly every restaurant offering a set menu comprising a starter, main course of meat or fish, a dessert and a glass of wine, a beer or a soft drink. Prices and quality vary, of course, but you should be able to eat well and substantially for around €7–12.

To get the most out of the cuisine in Barcelona, try to eat at the same time as the locals. Thus, breakfast only tends to be hearty when eaten mid-morning; earlier starts are more likely to feature coffee and biscuits. Lunch is the main meal of the day and eaten at about 2–3pm; dinner is a slightly lighter affair, served from around 9–10pm. If this seems like too long a wait, try having tapas with a drink, or visiting one of the many pastry shops around the city for an indulgently creamy cake.

El Fortuny

Carrer del Pintor Fortuny 31; tel: 93 317 98 92; Tue–Sun B, L and D; €

The easy-going atmosphere of a student café belies the high standard of the carefully executed French-influenced dishes available here.

La Reina del Raval

Rambla del Raval 5; tel: 93 443 36 55; Tue–Sat L and D, Sun L only; €–€€

With big windows looking on to the Rambla del Raval, this bright modern space has a young clientele, and features an eclectic menu with market ingredients. There is a gourmet menu, an *à la carte* and a daily lunchtime set menu, as well as tapas.

The Waterfront

Agua

Passeig Marítim 30; tel: 93 225 12 72; daily L and D; €€–€€€

Almost on the beach, with tables both indoor and out, the modern and attractive Agua gets very busy, especially at lunchtime, so booking is essential. Part of the Tragaluz group, it offers well-prepared fish and seafood, rice dishes such as risottos, and imaginative vegetarian dishes.

> Price guide for a three-course *à-la-carte* dinner for one with half a bottle of house wine:
>
> | | |
> |---|---|
> | €€€€ | over 60 euros |
> | €€€ | 30–60 euros |
> | €€ | 20–30 euros |
> | € | below 20 euros |

Barceloneta

Carrer de l'Escar 22; tel 93 221 21 11; daily L and D; €€€

The Barceloneta's outdoor terrace in a privileged position, jutting out above the fishing boats and smooth yachts of the marina Port Vell, makes this one of the most perfect places to have standard seafood dishes.

La Oca Mar

Espigó Bac de Roda, Platja Mar Bella; tel: 93 225 01 00; daily L and D; €€

This spectacular restaurant, situated right on the breakwater, virtually in the sea, serves a range of well-prepared seafood and local seasonal dishes.

Travi del Port

Moll de Gregal, Local 33, 1st floor; tel: 93 225 99 66; daily L and D; €€–€€€

In the Olympic Port, this dependable seafood restaurant prepares well-prepared, if fairly predictable, fish and shellfish. The views of the surrounding port are superb. Good entertainment for restless children is available nearby.

Xiringuíto Escribà

Avinguda del Litoral Mar 42, Platja del Bogatell; tel: 93 221 07 29; summer: daily L and D, winter: Tue–Sun L only; €€€

Lots of imaginative fish and rice dishes in this down-to-earth, family-run establishment, right by the beach. The Escribà family is renowned for chocolates and pastries, so the puddings are guaranteed to be marvellous.

Alkimia

Carrer de la Indústria 79; tel: 93 207
61 15; Mon–Fri L and D, Sat D only;
€€€

Near the Sagrada Família, this is a
shining example of the new talent in
Catalan cuisine. Young chef Jordi Vilà
is the alchemist in question, working
wonders on ordinary Catalan dishes
and converting them into something
extraordinary. Fast becoming one of
Barcelona's leading restaurants.

Casa Calvet

Carrer de Casp 48; tel: 93 412 40 12;
Mon–Sat L and D; €€€–€€€€

Located on the first floor of one of
Antoni Gaudí's first apartment buildings, Casa Calvet exudes elegant
Modernista ambience. The tables are
spaced well apart; some even occupy
private booth areas, and the excellent
Catalan menu is fairly priced.

El Caballito Blanco

Carrer de Mallorca 196; tel: 93 453
10 33; Tue–Sat L and D, Sun L only;
€€€

This is an old-fashioned, popular place
that always has a large number of
international and Catalan dishes to
choose from. The fresh ingredients are
selected from what is in season. It is a
relief to find places like this have
escaped being redesigned and
relaunched in 21st-century Barcelona.

Gorría

Carrer de la Diputació 421; tel: 93
245 11 64; Mon–Sat L and D; €€€

As genuine as the first day the Gorría
family opened this Basque restaurant
nearly 30 years ago. Daily deliveries
of fish from the north make it the perfect place to eat *bacalao a la vizcaína* or
other traditional Basque dishes.

Jaume de Provença

Carrer de Provença 88; tel: 93 430
00 29; Tue–Sat L and D, Sun L only;
€€€

A small restaurant with a country
flavour located near Sants station,
named after its innovative owner-chef
Jaume Barguès. It is still considered to
be among the best of the nouvelle cuisine restaurants in Barcelona and is
correspondingly popular.

L'Olive

Carrer de Balmes 47; tel: 93 452 19
90; Mon–Sat L and D, Sun L only;
€€€

L'Olive has long been considered a
fashionable place for classic Catalan
dishes such as *pa amb tomàquet*, *faves*
(stewed baby broad beans) and *escalivada* (grilled peppers and aubergines).
The slick new premises are not quite
as atmospheric as the original ones.

Tragaluz

Passatge de la Concepció 5; tel: 93
487 06 21; daily L and D; €€€

Barcelona's love affair with food is
vivid in this trendy, colourful restaurant in a tiny passageway off the
Passeig de Gràcia. The creative menu
extends to a selection of low-fat and
vegetarian dishes and a separate sushi
restaurant downstairs.

**Above from far
left:** the new and
old faces of dining
in Barcelona, at El
Rovell del Born
(Carrer Argentería
6) and El Quatre
Gats *(see p.35)*.

Seafood
Peix (fish) and
marisc (shellfish)
should not be
missed in
Barcelona; a *grael-
lada* (mixed grill)
allows you to
sample several
dishes at once and
is a good option
for two to share.
For paella, it is
worth going to a
good restaurant,
as cheap imitations
are usually dis-
appointing and not
representative of
the great seafood
on offer here.

CREDITS

Insight Step by Step Barcelona
Written by: Roger Williams
Series Editor: Clare Peel
Cartography Editor: James Macdonald
Picture Managers: Hilary Genin,
Steve Lawrence
Art Editor: Ian Spick
Production: Kenneth Chan
Editorial Director: Brian Bell
Photography by: Apa: Annabel Elston, Jon
Santa Cruz, Jeroen Sniders, Bill Wassman and
Gregory Wrona except: Alamy 21tl, 67tr, 98tr,
99tr; Corbis 2/3, 7tr, 7br, 11br, 12tr, 20tl, 20tr,
21tr, 28bl, 32tr, 36b, 66tr, 70tl, 71tl, 78bl, 80tl,
82tl, 88t, 89t, 90t, 91t, 91br, 100–1; Mike Mer-
chant 61tl; MNAC 22t, 76tr; Ingrid Morató 44l
(c, t, b); Photoasia 23t, 23b; Prisma Archivo
Fotográfico 22bl; Turisme de Barcelona/G. Foto
102, 112b; Turisme de Barcelona/J. Trullàs 112t.
Cover: main image: age fotostock/SuperStock;
front left: Stuart Pitkin/istock photo; front right:
Gregory Wrona/Apa.

Printed by: Insight Print Services (Pte) Ltd,
38 Joo Koon Road, Singapore 628990

First Edition 2008

DISTRIBUTION

Worldwide
**Apa Publications GmbH & Co. Verlag KG
(Singapore branch)**, 38 Joo Koon Road,
Singapore 628990
Tel: (65) 6865 1600
Fax: (65) 6861 6438

UK and Ireland
GeoCenter International Ltd
Meridian House, Churchill Way West,
Basingstoke, Hampshire, RG21 6YR
Tel: (44) 1256 817 987
Fax: (44) 1256 817 988

United States
Langenscheidt Publishers, Inc.
36–36 33rd Street, 4th Floor,
Long Island City, NY 11106
Tel: (1) 718 784 0055
Fax: (1) 718 784 0640

Australia
Universal Publishers
1 Waterloo Road, Macquarie Park, NSW 2113
Tel: (61) 2 9857 3700
Fax: (61) 2 9888 9074

New Zealand
Hema Maps New Zealand Ltd (HNZ)
Unit D, 24 Ra ORA Drive,
East Tamaki, Auckland
Tel: (64) 9 273 6459
Fax: (64) 9 273 6479

CONTACTING THE EDITORS

We would appreciate it if readers would alert us
to errors or outdated information by writing to
us at insight@apaguide.co.uk or Apa Publications,
PO Box 7910, London SE1 1WE, UK.

www.insightguides.com

INDEX